Struggling
FOR LIFE

How Your Tax Dollars and
Twisted Science Target the Unborn

Struggling
FOR LIFE

*How Your Tax Dollars and
Twisted Science Target the Unborn*

KELLY HOLLOWELL

Struggling for Life: How Your Tax Dollars and Twisted Science Target the Unborn
© 2006 Coral Ridge Ministries Media, Inc.

By Dr. Kelly Hollowell, Senior Analyst for the Center for Reclaiming America for Christ.

Sam Kastensmidt, News Analyst at the Center for Reclaiming America for Christ, provided extensive editorial and research assistance for chapter three, "Making a Bloody Fortune." His contribution is gratefully acknowledged.

Published by the Center for Reclaiming America for Christ, an outreach of Coral Ridge Ministries Media, Inc.

Printed in the United States of America.

Design: Roark Creative, www.roarkcreative.com

Center for Reclaiming America for Christ
P.O. Box 632
Fort Lauderdale, Florida 33302
1-877-SALT-USA (725-8872)
cfra@coralridge.org

CONTENTS

FOREWORD

I t is now 33 years since the U.S. Supreme Court first introduced the fabricated constitutionality of abortion. That decision has expanded far beyond its initial holding to become one of the most permissive abortion regimes of any Western nation. And still the unborn have never been in more danger than they are today for further abuse. Quite simply, they are targeted for death from conception until birth.

Through advances in technology, the scientific community seeks to destroy these young lives in order to harvest their body parts only days after conception. This twisted use of technology is cunningly masked and sympathetically packaged as a pursuit of cures. Later in development, all the way until birth, disturbing and distorted advances in feminist philosophy seek to destroy the unborn by selling another false bill of goods—that being the marketing of abortion as an expression of sexual freedom, liberation, and choice.

The combined fruit of this legal and cultural trend has led to the death of millions of the unborn—one child at a time. For those who have survived, it has produced a generation of youth that find little, if any, inherent value in human life. This is seen most brutally across the country in the terrifying rise of children callously taking the lives of parents, teachers, and even classmates over the most trivial of disagreements.

Is there anything that could make the killing of the unborn and its effects any worse? Just one thing—forcing the American people to pay for this killing with their tax dollars. That's right! Unbeknownst to most Americans, Planned Parenthood is getting rich off your tax dollars and mine. Naturally, they claim our money isn't used for abortion but for "other services to women," but that is the equivalent of paying the mortgage of a drug addict and claiming you don't support their habit.

The good news is that we can end this horrible misuse of our tax dollars and quash the life-destroying effects of this cultural trend. Together we can hasten the day when unborn children are both protected in law and welcomed in life no matter the circumstances of their conception or condition.

We can begin by following the wise counsel offered by Dr. Kelly Hollowell in this highly readable book. Dr. Hollowell, a Senior Bioethics Strategist for our Center for Reclaiming America for Christ, speaks with expertise and from personal experience on the role of medical technology in the life debate and offers an innovative "L.I.F.E." formula for winning the battle for the unborn. The chapter on how America's leading abortion provider, Planned Parenthood, has convinced lawmakers to provide an increasing amount of your tax dollars to finance its pro-abortion agenda is both illuminating and infuriating.

Dr. Hollowell is a Ph.D. in molecular and cellular pharmacology, an attorney, and most importantly, a mother of two young children, one with Down syndrome. That diagnosis, which came when Dr. Hollowell was four months pregnant with Victoria, is a death sentence for most unborn with Down syndrome. An astonishing 80 percent of children diagnosed in utero with Down syndrome are killed before they draw their first breath.

But today, Victoria is a beautiful, miraculously healthy, vibrantly alive, and beloved little girl who testifies to her parents' pro-life conviction. Down syndrome, as the Hollowells have discovered, is a genetic anomaly that encodes for love.

May God bless you as you read *Struggling for Life* and become more well-informed and better equipped to advance the cause of life.

D. James Kennedy, Ph.D.
President and Founder
Center for Reclaiming America for Christ

Chapter 1

Encoded for Love

I received a call late one September afternoon from a colleague-in-arms asking me for help. He wanted me to write the following true story, which has been buried by a conspiracy of silence rooted in political and media bias.

The story is about an incredibly loving young girl named Christin Gilbert. A very active high school graduate and a beloved member of her softball team and community, she was sweet beyond the norm, as so often is the case for children with her diagnosis. She had Down syndrome.

I have heard it said, anecdotally, that the extra chromosome which characterizes Trisomy 21, encodes for love. For those of you blessed enough to know anyone with Down syndrome, you will likely agree. There is simply something about these gifted children that reminds us all of what really matters in life, no matter how busy or complicated our lives appear. Senator Sam Brownback (R-KS) made just that point during the nomination hearing for now-Chief Justice of the U.S. Supreme Court John Roberts.

Brownback spoke on the effects of *Roe v. Wade*—of the 40 million children who have died—and then of children diagnosed with a disability while still in the womb. For example, the records show that more than 80 percent of all children diagnosed with Down syndrome are killed before they are born.[1] This tragedy is compounded by the fact that a literal waiting list of people exists to adopt these children. Their deaths are a great loss not only to biological mothers and families, but to society as a whole.

By way of personal experience, Senator Brownback spoke of a young man named Jimmy, diagnosed with Down syndrome, who operates an elevator in the Senate building.

> BROWNBACK: His warm smile welcomes us every day. We're a better body for him. He told me the other day —he frequently gives me a hug in the elevator afterwards. I know he does Senator Hatch often, too, who kindly gives him ties, some of which I question the taste of, Orrin...
> (LAUGHTER)
> ... but he kindly gives ties.
> HATCH: It doesn't have to get personal...
> (LAUGHTER)
> BROWNBACK: Jimmy said to me the other day, after

he hugged me, "Shhh, don't tell my supervisor. They're telling me I'm hugging too many people."

(LAUGHTER)

BROWNBACK: And, yet, we're ennobled by him and what he does and how he lifts up our humanity, and 80 to 90 percent of the kids in this country like Jimmy never get here. What does that do to us? What does that say about us?[2]

According to these statistics, those like Jimmy and Christin, who are given a chance at life, are exceptions to the general rule and the trend to kill the unborn diagnosed with a disability. Sadly, for Christin things unexpectedly changed in 2005. In January of that year, Christin was not only sexually assaulted but, remarkably, became pregnant. No one seems sure how frequently young women diagnosed with Down syndrome become pregnant. According to the experts I consulted, the numbers are likely too rare for an official count. One thing is sure: of those becoming pregnant, complications are likely to exist—especially if the child shares the mother's genetic diagnosis.

In Christin's case, and according to well-documented resources, she was taken by her family, at 28 weeks pregnant, to Wichita, Kansas, to the infamous abortion clinic of Dr. George Tiller.[3] At that time one drug was administered to kill the baby and another drug to open her cervix for delivery or removal of the dead baby. After starting the procedure, which normally takes three to four days, Christin was sent to a local hotel to begin her labor.

Somewhat surprisingly, she returned to the clinic the next day; the abortion procedure was completed, and she was once again told to return to her hotel room. Immediately, her condition began to deteriorate. When she returned to the clinic, her symptoms were misdiagnosed as dehydration. She was given an IV and again sent back to her hotel, where she began having episodes of vomiting and unconsciousness. She was advised to return to the clinic, where she became unresponsive. By this time Christin was in serious trouble. According to one doctor who reviewed her autopsy report, she was "bleeding and oozing from every orifice of her body."

A clinic employee called 911. More worried about the clinic's image than Christin's life, the employee begged the dispatcher to turn off the lights and sirens of the ambulance. In compliance, the ambulance arrived quietly and took Christin to the emergency room at a local medical center, but it was too late. Christin died. According to the medical examiner's report, her horrifying and painful death was a direct result of the abortion. What's worse, it could have been prevented, if not for the misdiagnosis and slow response of the abortion clinic staff.

As I read over the detailed timeline of her experience, I had to wonder how much Christin understood of what was happening to her during those painful and frightening hours leading to her death and the death of her baby. Down's Syndrome is frequently accompanied by mental disability.

This sweet and precious little girl was sexually assaulted, her baby was killed (likely without her consent), then she herself suffered and died a brutal and painful end. All without any news coverage or public outcry.

God help us for not protecting the most precious and vulnerable among us. I can only repeat the questions asked by Senator Brownback. "What does that do to us? What does that say about us?"

Down Syndrome Hits Home

This raises the question, "How do we in America measure the value of life?" Is it quality, quantity, or something else? A national debate over just such questions poignantly erupted in early 2005 during the life-and-death legal struggle on behalf of Terri Schiavo.

This subject strikes a particularly strong and personal chord in me. I have always believed in the sanctity of human life—both in situations like the one endured by Terri as well as those related to the unborn. This matter of the value of human life applies in a very personal way, because in October 2004, my own little girl was diagnosed *in utero* with Down syndrome.

The link between this personal situation and Terri Schiavo lies in the statistics I shared earlier. Some 80 percent of all children like my daughter are sentenced to death and killed in the womb. This startling fact brings tears to my eyes as I look at the precious face of my beautiful little girl. How did we as a nation ever arrive at a place where the only value life has is that assigned by Hollywood, academia, or utilitarian standards?

Patricia E. Bauer suggested in a *Washington Post* commentary that prenatal testing is transforming the right to abort a disabled child into a "duty." As the mother of a child with Down syndrome, she has struggled with America's view of the disabled.

She writes:

> As Margaret bounces through life, especially out here in the land of the perfect body, I see the way people look at her: curious, surprised, sometimes wary, occasionally disapproving or alarmed. I know that most women of childbearing age that we may encounter have judged her and her cohort, and have found their lives to be not worth living.

To them, Margaret falls into the category of avoidable human suffering. At best, a tragic mistake. At worst, a living embodiment of the pro-life movement. Less than human. A drain on society. That someone I love is regarded this way is unspeakably painful to me.[4]

She closes with a poignant question about the obvious, but never talked about hypocrisy of the liberal agenda. Do they actually care more about preserving the rights of people with a disability or preserving their own right to ensure that no one with disabilities will be born into their families? Based on abortion statistics for children diagnosed with disabilities, the answer could not be more obvious. I wonder how it would affect their public image to have that ugly truth exposed.

Surely, it goes without saying that these mindsets are a tragic reflection of the true shallowness of our culture and our preoccupation with worldly perfection. What's worse is that the exercise of these beliefs is seen at both ends of the spectrum of life.

In Terri Schiavo, we had a brain-injured woman whose parents were fighting for her life and willing to spend their lives meeting the continuing needs of their daughter. They were opposed by Terri's husband. He insisted that Terri wanted to die.

As for Terri's physical condition, there were many conflicting reports. Some say she was responsive and could have been rehabilitated. Others say she was non-responsive and rehabilitation was impossible. But who can really predict the future or the progression of her diagnosis, especially in light of rapidly advancing medicine? Stories of patients waking after years spent in a coma or permanent vegetative state are growing more and more commonplace. And experts agree that they understand very little about brain damage and repair processes.

Again, from my personal experience, consider my daughter Victoria, diagnosed with Down syndrome. When I was 16 weeks pregnant, my husband and I were specifically warned of anomalies on both her heart and kidney, which were revealed by ultrasound.

For those who don't know, Down syndrome is associated with a number of major malformations. Approximately half of Down syndrome children are born with a heart defect, and a great many others are born with intestinal complications—both of which can require surgery upon birth.

Naturally, I was afraid of the unknown and the myriad of major and minor complications associated with Down syndrome. To the doctors' surprise, both anomalies—tracked by 4D-ultrasound—simply disappeared with time. Then at eight months into my pregnancy another threat arose. I was told I had elevated levels of amniotic fluid known as polyhydramnios. According to more than one source, congenital defects are the cause of polyhydramnios.[5] But this, too, disappeared in time, becoming nothing more than a false alarm.

My point is this. There were and still are many threats to the overall health of my daughter. And there were many times that someone who did not believe in the sanctity of human life might have been driven by "quality of life" arguments and fear to end Victoria's life in the womb.

Truth is, as a pro-life advocate I hear arguments like these all the time. Sadly, just such arguments were successfully made to end Terri Schiavo's life.

These developments have only served to strengthen my resolve and response to the quality of life arguments. That is to say, "There are no sure-fire predictors for the meaning, quality, or quantity of anyone's life."

For example—although my daughter Victoria has Down syndrome, she is in every way the picture of health. Examples like hers should warn anyone against making a life-and-death decision for anyone or projecting a sliding scale of value onto another human life, whether born or unborn.

According to this nation's founding principles and biblical teaching, life is unquestionably sacred and has inherent value. It is also in many ways completely unpredictable and often produces results contrary to the predictions made by "experts," particularly when the power of prayer is factored in. Of course, for those scientific elites who discount God, the idea of prayer is just a myth held onto by the common folk—something about which to smile and maybe roll their eyes. Let's examine these scientific elites and see where they are attempting to take us.

Chapter 2

Mad Scientists

L et me introduce you to the mad scientists of the academic elite. These are, under the best circumstances, well-educated, by-the-book, no-room-for-God/this is science physicians. Under the worst circumstances, these are condescending, know-it-all, chronically self-absorbed demigods who cast off ethical restraint as something only for the bourgeoisie. Let's take a look for a moment at the Dr. Jekylls among us. This will help us better assess the true nature of the battleground over issues of life in America.

In March 2004, the director of the University of California, Los Angeles, Willed-Body Program was arrested for allegedly stealing body parts from the medical school.[6] "Mr. Creepy Dude" says he cut up hundreds of cadavers and sold the pieces to large research corporations, with the knowledge of UCLA officials. Evidently, the trade in human body parts is a booming industry thought to be worth half a billion dollars a year and growing.

The question is: How has the once noble scientific profession sunk to such lows in moral depravity and unethical conduct? The answer is a self-regulated and ego-driven academic community of scientists who think themselves above the reproach of laymen and the moral laws that bind the rest of culture and society. I know this for a fact. I was there.

For six long years I worked in graduate school earning my Ph.D. in molecular and cellular pharmacology. Unexpectedly, an experience with the dark side of scientific research occurred as I neared completion of my thesis.

Most people don't know that to obtain a Ph.D. in science, candidates need to make a contribution to the body of science as a whole. That contribution often equates to a discovery of some kind. For me, the contribution was the discovery of a new protein expressed only in the developing brain.

After the discovery of this new protein, I entered the office of my mentor, thinking all that was left was to write my thesis and a paper for publication. To my surprise, he chastised me for that presumption. Speaking critically, he said, "Scientific research is not intended to benefit animals, but people."

The look of confusion on my face prompted his next instruction, which was to conduct a final experiment in search of the human counterpart to my newly discovered protein. He strongly suggested that this final experiment could secure publication in a more prominent scientific journal. (Until that point I had only used animal models.)

My heart and shoulders sank at the prospect of even one more set of experiments, but what he said made sense. So I asked him what to do. He said to call the tissue bank across the street for fetal tissue. "You'll need brain, heart, liver, lung, and kidney."

Ten minutes later I stood in a dimly lit laboratory staring into a large trunk-like freezer, as the technician pulled out test tubes with the requested fetal tissue. I confirmed my order and shoved the samples into a bucket of dry ice I had brought for transport. Tissue in hand, I bounded back to my own laboratory to finish the last of my thesis experiments.

Because I lived a predominantly secular life at the time, I gave no thought to the source of that tissue or its moral implications. I was solely focused on completing my thesis work and receiving my Ph.D. In short order, I forgot the final experiments entirely.

I forgot, that is, until years later when I revisited the published text of my thesis. I flipped through the pages, casually refreshing my memory of the work I accomplished until I came to the final chapter. It was then, with horror, that I relived the final days of my research—realizing at long last what I had done. I realized for the first time my complicity in the vacuous immorality of the research I conducted—and that is still being conducted every day.

This sort of self-realization rarely occurs. Too many scientists remain forever myopic, their entire focus on new discovery and the prestige it brings. Worse, to keep their hands clean and their positions secure, they sometimes deliberately and strategically place "yes men" in positions like my supplier, who was similarly situated to the director of the UCLA Willed-Body Program.

In the UCLA case, lurking behind the prestigious title was nothing more than a non-academic technician trained as a mortician. He and others like him enter rooms of cadavers with a tray and a hacksaw. Bodies are dismembered; their parts are sorted and sold to the tissue and organ bank industries. The body parts are then used for commercial research and/or to supply colleagues in research (like me) with a ready supply of tissue for human experimentation. This is done with donated cadavers from John and Jane Doe and, obviously, aborted babies.

The problem is that the world of scientific research is so competitive that few ever ask the source of human tissue. Most researchers are just grateful to obtain the tissue they need to get their research published.

So what is the most frequently exercised ethic behind this kind of work? There is none. There is only goal-oriented, deadline-driven or ego-driven obsession. Ethical considerations are a low priority, if they exist at all. Admittedly, there are some stopgap measures provided through limits in federal funding. There are, however, few if any limits on privately funded research.

The reality is that the incident at UCLA is a drop in the proverbial bucket of the black market trade in human body parts. This is a dark but integral part of modern scientific research that goes largely unnoticed because it is cloaked by the fancy titles, sterile labs and white coats of the academic elite.

No Ethical Barriers

Even now scientists are secretly pushing forward in their agenda to scale the highest scientific mountains without regard for ethical restraint. Consider that in February of 2004 a literal "cookbook" for human cloning was released. It wasn't titled that way, so as not to alarm the non-scientific community or stir protest to this kind of research. Rather it read like any other significant and acceptable scientific advance in a peer reviewed journal:

> We report the derivation of a pluripotent embryonic stem cell line (SCNT-hES-1) from a cloned human blastocyst.[7]

With this scientific and innocuous-sounding statement, Korean researchers actually announced that they had created and killed several human clones for the purpose of extracting their stem cells. Even worse, their detailed recipe on how to create human embryos by cloning was published in the journal *Science*. It has since been alleged that this research was fraudulent but, if accurate, this recipe, intended to advance therapeutic cloning, will undoubtedly also advance reproductive cloning. After all, it has been placed in the hands of every scientist, including any nut case with access to a laboratory. Remember the Raelians?

According to one report, when fertility laboratories fertilize eggs and grow embryos to the same developmental stage as the Korean embryo clones, 40 to 60 percent end up as babies when implanted. That means a human clone may be born in the very near future.

Despite these ominous consequences, the reason for doing this kind of research is always the same. Proponents say, "This research will aid in the treatment of disease, such as leukemia and Parkinson's. It has a wide range of applications in the medical and related fields. And the potential benefits outweigh the potential danger that human life itself will be manipulated." The Korean researchers went one step further, claiming they conducted this research, despite the controversy, because they are scientists and think it is their obligation.

Translation: These doctors and scientists are hiding behind the noble curtain of healing our parents from Parkinson's disease and our children from leukemia, but they are destroying human life in the process. That's called human sacrifice. So at the very least, let's dispense with all the false piety and technical jargon.

We all know by now that there are two forms of human cloning: reproductive and therapeutic. The goal of reproductive cloning is to create and give birth to a baby. (Virtually no one supports this publicly.) The goal of therapeutic cloning is to create a baby who will be sacrificed for his or her body parts, specifically embryonic stem cells that will be used for research and/or treatment.

Both forms of cloning begin with a procedure called somatic cell nuclear transfer. This technique was first used by the creators of Dolly, the sheep, and now by the Korean scientists. In both reproductive cloning and therapeutic cloning, a life is created. This is an undisputed fact.

Obviously, there has never been a greater need to protest the current direction of this unethical research. But this is not a rejection of technological advance. In fact, nearly all Americans recognize and applaud advances in science and medicine, such as transplant surgery, cancer treatment, and ironically, adult stem cell research that improve our health and lives. But technological advance in a civilized society must preserve human dignity by staying within biblical ethical limits and moral boundaries.

In response to "advances" in human cloning specifically, and medical technology generally, it's time for average Americans to cowboy-up and confront the mindset of scientists who view themselves as above all ethical and moral limits. It means quashing the idea that there are no limits on what they do in the name of science. It means enforcing the idea that non-scientists have a say in the research scientists conduct and experiments they pursue. Scientists have a duty beyond themselves and discovery. They have a duty to comply with the ethical and moral limits that define us as a culture and nation.

Like many other Americans, I believe that efforts to create human beings by cloning marks a new threshold in moral depravity, opening the floodgates to unspeakable human-rights violations and grisly human experimentation on our unborn children. It is not only a decisive step toward turning human reproduction into a manufacturing process, but it transforms the mystery and majesty of life into a mere malleable and marketable commodity.

The only measure likely to distance America from countries like Korea is to pass federal legislation, or at least to counteract immoral state laws such as the "clone and kill" bill passed in New Jersey. This bill actually allows the creation of cloned human embryos that can be implanted into a woman's womb and then destroyed at any point during their development for use in scientific research. As expected, former New Jersey Governor Jim McGreevey signed the bill into law, January 4, 2004, making it the most extreme law ever passed regarding human cloning and embryonic stem cell research.[8]

Supporters say it is an innocuous and forward-looking measure opposed only by extremists. But the new statute will have morally disastrous effects. Most notably, it creates a commercial market for the body parts of unborn children. It authorizes the commercial traffic of cloned children and will inevitably lead to contracts between cloning entrepreneurs and gestating women.

The law does make cloning a crime of the first degree. But cloning is defined in an unprecedented way: "cultivating" the cell "through the egg, embryo, fetal, and newborn stages into a new human individual." That means the crime of cloning would not occur until a cloned child was possibly weeks or months old. That further means that the only way to avoid the crime of cloning would be to kill the child—even after birth.

Now defenders might say that cloned children would not be allowed to develop to the newborn stage. The problem is that no woman contracted to carry a cloned child could be forced to abort the child. Therefore, if the woman changes her mind while carrying the child and decides to forego abortion, a cloned child would be born.

These are just a few of the problems opponents of therapeutic cloning and embryonic stem cell research fear. They are also concerned by the obvious attempt to further expand our current abortion laws. At present we can kill a child at any point in the womb. Even partial birth abortion bans have been challenged as unconstitutional. So even though a child is capable of living outside the mother's womb, his or her life may be taken by the hand of his or her own mother moments before natural birth. At the other end of the pregnancy spectrum, scientists are finding ways through the administration of prescription drugs for do-it yourself abortions intended to kill unborn children hours and days after they are created.

These drugs are so dangerous that some pharmacists are refusing to dispense them. As a result, they are oftentimes losing their jobs. This is yet another way that ethically unbound medical technology is creating new controversy in the long-standing abortion debate.

Abortion Pills

The prescription drug for at-home abortions is called the "morning-after pill." It is also marketed by the innocuous-sounding name of "Plan B." This is a newly available abortifacient often confused with RU-486. The "morning-after pill" is also called the "emergency contraceptive" and is designed to address the "oops" factor. As in "Oops, I didn't take or use any contraceptive," or "Oops, I didn't expect to have sex," or "Oops, the relationship didn't last—so the baby has to go."

All of these afterthoughts are, of course, the consequence of casual sex. The answer, we're told by the secularists, is not abstinence, self-control, forethought or maternal responsibility—rather it is the *emergency* contraceptive that is taken *after* sex in the hope of preventing pregnancy.

The morning-after pills are essentially very high multiple dosages of birth-control pills taken within 72 hours of sexual relations. They work by preventing ovulation or implantation. When they successfully prevent ovulation, pregnancy will not occur. In other words, there is no egg to fertilize. If the woman becomes pregnant, the pill blocks the embryo from implanting into the mother's womb, causing an abortion of the early embryo.

By contrast, RU-486 is a pill specifically designed to abort an older more developed baby—not prevent ovulation or implantation. This pill regimen, approved by the Food and Drug Administration just four years ago, has resulted in countless deaths of women through blood loss, bacterial infection, and heart attacks.

This drug can be taken during the first nine weeks of pregnancy. In this regimen, a woman is given the RU-486 pills, followed two days later with a dose of a prostaglandin. This combination induces powerful uterine contractions to expel the baby from the womb.

The presently debated difference between morning-after pills and RU-486 is that administration of RU-486 is performed under medical supervision at authorized medical centers. The morning-after pill is provided to women through a prescription. This allows the woman to take the drug and carry out an unmonitored and unsupervised abortion at home.

The question is: "Should a pharmacist be forced to participate in the abortion of a child by filling a prescription for these drugs?"

The obvious problem for pro-life pharmacists is that they recognize life begins at conception. That means they cannot, in good conscience, dispense drugs that work after an egg is fertilized because that, in effect, ends a life. Naturally, pro-life groups defend these pharmacists, claiming they should be allowed to exercise their conscience and opt out of dispensing these drugs.

The counterargument by abortion advocates is that any pharmacist unwilling to care for a woman's total health should not be a pharmacist at all. However, no one forces a physician to participate in abortions. Shouldn't the same logic and standards apply to pharmacists as it does doctors who oppose abortion, based on moral or religious convictions?

Of course, the quick fix is quite simple. Objecting pharmacists can refer these customers to another pharmacist, or even another store. Unfortunately, there are innumerable complications on the horizon of this immediate issue.

Specifically, there is the growing ease with which we dispose of our unborn children in our culture. Technology offers a myriad of ways to eliminate them from the womb. Some are obvious and intentional, and some are not.

For example, even some contraceptives can, at times, abort an early embryo, even though they are not prescribed for that purpose. Additionally, the very use of fertility drugs by women who want children often leads to abortion through selective reduction. Even standard in vitro fertilization procedures involve the sacrifice of the unborn.

These examples make clear that as science and medicine continue to advance, the moral implications of reproductive technologies should be addressed—but by whom and when? Perhaps the doctors who line their pockets with the proceeds of these procedures aren't the only people to ask for guidance. Maybe this is a job for the Church; but when was the last time issues like these were discussed with your congregation?

As to the dispensing of do-it-yourself abortion pills, for now it appears to be a matter of policy for individual pharmacists or pharmacies. But it is of particular interest that Planned Parenthood is a very interested party in the sale of the morning after pill. In fact the organization is rather forcefully pushing for FDA approval to make the morning after pill available not only by prescription, but also as an over-the-counter drug.

According to Jim Sedlak, the director of STOPP International (Stamp Out Planned Parenthood), a group that monitors Planned Parenthood, "this would not only represent an ideological victory for Planned Parenthood Federation of America, but it would also generate a financial windfall. Because of a series of shrewd business agreements, the organization could be in position to make a minimum profit of $100 million over a five-year period from Plan B sales if the FDA gives the go-ahead for over-the-counter distribution."[9] But even if the FDA turns down over-the-counter status, Planned Parenthood has already turned a huge profit on the morning after pill by making equity investments in and internal price-fixing arrangements with the corporation that brings the pill to the market.

This sweetheart financial arrangement is not the only way Planned Parenthood stands to make profits. It is an organization that is already living high on the hog at our expense. In its 2003-2004 annual report, Planned Parenthood announced that it had received more than $265 million in government grants and contracts during its fiscal year ending June 30, 2004.[10] Let's take a little closer look at this outrageous use of taxpayer money.

Chapter 3

Making a Bloody Fortune

I magine a country that forced its citizens to fund an organization which, by itself, was the third leading cause of death in
that nation.[11] In addition to operating an industry of death,
imagine that this organization targeted communities based on race,
fought tooth and nail to undermine parental rights, and exposed
teens to the most debauched forms of sexual perversion imaginable.

Well, that is no imaginary nation. In fact, you are living in it, if you call America your home.

In 2003, the Planned Parenthood Federation of America ended the lives of 244,628 unborn babies—making the organization more deadly than leukemia, brain cancer, skin cancer,[12] diabetes,[13] car accidents,[14] Alzheimer's disease,[15] and HIV/AIDS[16] combined.

What is more shocking is that due to the irresponsibility, ignorance, or cowardice of our elected officials, America's taxpayers have been forced to finance a substantial portion of this group's grotesque agenda. As already mentioned, Planned Parenthood received more than $265 million in government grants and contracts during its fiscal year ending June 30, 2004.[17]

Follow the Money

Tragically, this abuse of taxpayer dollars is nothing new! In the seven years after June 30, 1997, Planned Parenthood received more than $1.49 billion from American taxpayers.[18] So how is it using the money? In its annual reports, the organization admits that it performed 1,398,574 abortions from 1997 to 2003.[19] Of course, Planned Parenthood claims that it does not use taxpayer funds to finance abortion procedures, but uses those funds for "other services" they provide. This claim is logically absurd.

Would the U.S. government have financed the "good works" (education, building bridges, etc.) of the Nazi regime—so long as the Nazis promised not to use those funds for purposes of destroying human life in its concentration camps? Common sense dictates the answer—"NO!"

I mean even if Nazis *did not* use the tax dollars directly for an evil like genocide, such funding would free up their other finances, allowing them to invest more in their openly evil agenda. Likewise, we should not support Planned Parenthood with our tax dollars. As it stands, they not only achieve their goals and objectives, but also accumulate profits in the hundreds of millions of dollars.

But we do support Planned Parenthood with our taxes. In fact, America's unsuspecting taxpayers have not only financed the abortion industry agenda, we *have* helped Planned Parenthood accumulate profits of more than $350 million in just seven years.[20] That's right, this "nonprofit" tax-funded organization has run a huge surplus for the last seven years (see diagram 1).

FISCAL YEAR	PPFA PROFITS
2003-2004	$ 35.2 million
2002-2003	$ 36.6 million
2001-2002	$ 12.2 million
2000-2001	$ 38.9 million
1999-2000	$ 59.5 million
1998-1999	$125.8 million
1997-1998	$ 42.1 million

diagram 1

It's hard not to wonder why an organization that has mounted profits of $350 million needs additional government grants. Despite more conservative leadership in Washington, government grants and contracts continue to be a large and growing portion of Planned Parenthood's revenue, growing from $165 million in 1997-98 to more than $265 million in 2003-04[21] (see diagram 2).

FISCAL YEAR	TOTAL REVENUE	GOV'T. GRANTS AND CONTRACTS
2003-2004	$810.0 million	$265.2 million
2002-2003	$766.6 million	$254.4 million
2001-2002	$692.5 million	$240.9 million
2000-2001	$672.6 million	$202.7 million
1999-2000	$627.2 million	$187.3 million
1998-1999	$660.7 million	$176.5 million
1997-1998	$554.2 million	$165.0 million

diagram 2

To measure the significance of such funding, compare government grants to Planned Parenthood with allocations in the Department of Homeland Security Appropriations Act of 2005.[22]

The U.S. government sent more money to Planned Parenthood during its 2003-2004 fiscal year than the $126 million appropriated for the Container Security Initiative (for inspecting cargo when foreign ships reach our shores); the $67.4 million for the National Cyber Security Division (for protecting America from computer hackers and cyber-terrorists); the $15 million for the National Incident Management System (for coordinating federal, state, and local responses for domestic incidences); and the $20 million earmarked for the National Disaster Medical System (which allows FEMA to run planning exercises associated with medical surge capabilities).[23]

Federal funding for Planned Parenthood not only exceeds each of these initiatives individually; it exceeds the funding for all of these initiatives combined!

Millions for Lobbying

Next consider that with the help of taxpayers, the organization has spent more than $193 million to influence public policy in the seven years ending June 30, 2004. This is more money than the Federal Elections Commission allotted to either George W. Bush or John Kerry during their 2004 Presidential campaigns.[24] Frankly, Planned Parenthood's annual spending on public policy matters is nothing short of astonishing (see diagram 3).

FISCAL YEAR	PUBLIC POLICY
2003-2004	$39.4 million
2002-2003	$39.5 million
2001-2002	$36.8 million
2000-2001	$24.5 million
1999-2000	$20.9 million
1998-1999	$20.3 million
1997-1998	$11.8 million

diagram 3

As a result of such financial strength, Planned Parenthood wields enormous influence at both the state and federal levels. *Fortune* magazine twice named Planned Parenthood one of the most powerful lobbying groups in America.[25]

Planned Parenthood flexes its political muscle by vehement opposition to many of President Bush's judicial nominees, arguing that they are "out of the mainstream." Meanwhile, it ardently promotes an agenda that very few Americans embrace. For example, they advocate unrestricted access to abortion, usurpation of parental rights, distributing condoms in schools, government funding of domestic and international abortions, forcing pro-life pharmacists to distribute abortion-inducing drugs, and much more.

In addition to its efforts to influence legislation at both the state and federal levels, Planned Parenthood has used its massive financial war chest to advance its agenda via activist courts and ideologically driven judges.

Using the Courts

Planned Parenthood appeals to unelected, unaccountable judges to legislate new policies from the bench—essentially force-feeding a destructive agenda down the throats of non-consenting Americans. To that end, Planned Parenthood has filed hundreds of lawsuits throughout the nation, exerting tremendous influence in the liberalization of American jurisprudence.

For example, Planned Parenthood has argued cases in front of the U.S. Supreme Court seeking to overturn state laws requiring parental consent (*Planned Parenthood of Central Missouri v. Danforth*, 1976); to force state Medicaid programs to fund abortion procedures (*Perdue v. Planned Parenthood of Alaska*, 2000); to overturn state laws requiring hospitalization for women who obtain abortions after the first trimester (*Planned Parenthood of Kansas City v. Ashcroft*, 1983); to defend *Roe v. Wade*, and to overturn state laws requiring married women to inform their husbands of planned abortions (*Planned Parenthood v. Casey*, 1992); and even to oppose simple informed consent laws requiring abortionists to inform women of the risks associated with abortion (*Planned Parenthood v. State of Montana*, 1999).

More recently, Planned Parenthood filed a federal lawsuit to strike down the Partial-Birth Abortion Ban Act of 2003. Incredibly, in the case *Planned Parenthood Federation of America v. Ashcroft* (2004), Planned Parenthood succeeded in finding one federal judge who was willing to dismiss the representative voice of the American people. U.S. District Judge Phyllis J. Hamilton struck down the ban—writing in her opinion that it was "irrelevant" whether these partially born babies experienced pain as abortionists mercilessly thrust scissors through the back of their skulls.[26]

Planned Parenthood also seems intent on undermining parental rights. In the case of *Ayotte v. Planned Parenthood of Northern New England*, Planned Parenthood sought to overturn a New Hampshire law which simply required abortionists to *notify* a minor's parent 48 hours before performing an abortion. Though parental consent is required before a minor can get a tattoo or even receive an aspirin from a school nurse, Planned Parenthood convinced the First U.S. Circuit Court of Appeals that New Hampshire's parental notification law placed an "undue burden" on the minor's "right" to abortion.[27]

By filling the financial coffers of Planned Parenthood, American taxpayers help to make these suits possible. But the tentacle arms of Planned Parenthood don't end with access to our wallets. It is much more sinister than that. The truth is that Planned Parenthood has our very children in its sights.

Sexualizing America's Children

Most people know that Planned Parenthood wants to deny parents their role in guiding their teenage daughters through a decision that will impact the rest of their entire lives. It also targets youth directly by cheapening the perceived sanctity of sexual relationships among teens. And what do you know? It is at our expense. In only seven fiscal years—with more than $1.49 billion in government grants and contracts—Planned Parenthood has spent more than $248 million on sexuality education (see diagram 4).[28]

FISCAL YEAR	SEXUALITY EDUCATION
2003-2004	$44.2 million
2002-2003	$42.1 million
2001-2002	$40.7 million
2000-2001	$34.3 million
1999-2000	$31.8 million
1998-1999	$27.2 million
1997-1998	$27.8 million

diagram 4

You might think this a good thing, but it's not. While many opponents of abstinence-only education argue that comprehensive sexuality education is the only responsible option to prevent pregnancy and disease, very few people could justify the debauched sexual agenda advanced by Planned Parenthood. For instance, Planned Parenthood's online outreach to teenagers (www.teenwire.com) is nothing short of scandalous.

The website is so raunchy that South Dakota Governor Mike Rounds and the State Library Board rightly insisted that a simple link to the website be removed from the state library homepage.[29] After all, how many parents would appreciate the fact that Planned Parenthood is offering their teenage daughters information about the nutritional value of semen? Why do teens need to know that "a tablespoon of semen contains approximately six calories," and "all kinds of chemicals and minerals, including water, sugar, calcium, chlorine, magnesium, nitrogen, vitamin B12, and zinc."[30]

Planned Parenthood's appalling website actually provides teens with step-by-step instructions on how they can perform oral sex or "enjoy anal sex."[31] The website even offers a vivid description of what happens to semen after two people engage in sodomy.[32]

In addition, while Planned Parenthood claims that it supports abstinence, its website teaches children that "the definition of virginity leaves lots of room for interpretation."[33] In fact, rather than promoting the absolute benefits of abstinence, Planned Parenthood advises teens: "Everyone has different values about sexual experience. What's right for one person may not be right for another. In any case, having lots of experience doesn't make someone a 'slut'... Whether you've been around the block a few times or you're just starting out down that road, there's no such thing as the 'perfect' level of experience."[34]

Does this sound like a group trumpeting the merits of abstinence?

Indeed, Planned Parenthood seems more interested in diminishing the sanctity of sexual relationships. At every turn, the organization appears to be more infatuated with cheap avenues of sexual gratification than teaching children about the beautiful purpose of sex and the enormous responsibility that accompanies it. With these lessons utterly neglected, it is no accident that many Americans now treat pregnancy as an inconvenience rather than a beautiful miracle of God's grace. One Planned Parenthood resource actually advised its readers: "Don't rob yourself of joy by focusing on old-fashioned ideas about what's 'normal' or 'nice.'"[35]

Planned Parenthood of Canada even produced a nationally aired television commercial, entitled "Groovy New Feelings," featuring two actors dressed as male and female sexual organs. These two actors rush on stage in front of an auditorium filled with kids, and they proceeded to gyrate against one another. Meanwhile, other adult performers cheer and chant sexual encouragements, which are too vulgar to repeat. Yet, the organization claims that the commercial was designed to "let youth know that there are places to get accurate non-judgmental answers to sexual health questions."[36]

Thankfully, America's parents do not yet tolerate such antics! And because they refuse to stand for such scandalous lessons, Planned Parenthood has sometimes refused to allow parents inside of its "sexual health" conferences.

Off Limits to Parents

In 2004, Planned Parenthood hosted a conference in Waco, Texas, where parents were forbidden to attend. Inside, the organization distributed a controversial sex education book to children in grades 7-9. The book, *It's Perfectly Normal*, includes graphic illustrations of various sex acts, a boy putting on a condom, explanations of risqué sexual positions, discussions on homosexuality, tips for masturbation, and a list of nine reasons to have an abortion.[37]

Planned Parenthood holds these types of conferences, claiming that it is doing a service for the community, but this service always seems to involve some form of propagandizing or perversion. For instance, Planned Parenthood hosted a booth at the Jackson County, Oregon, fair. Rather than using the opportunity to share the positives of abstinence with young children, Planned Parenthood was reprimanded by the fair's manager for distributing condom necklaces to passing kids. Planned Parenthood officials later told reporters that they were simply "talking about condoms and being safe."[38]

As the nation's leading abortion performer continues to "talk about condoms and being safe," a recent study showed that the "strength" and "reliability" of Planned Parenthood condoms were actually rated "poor." The February 2005 edition of *Consumer Reports* reviewed 23 different condoms, and Planned Parenthood's Honeydew condom ranked dead last! The organization's "Colors" condom ranked second to last![39] No worries for Planned Parenthood. After all, failed contraceptives only facilitate a greater demand for abortion. Even the Alan Guttmacher Institute, founded in 1968 as a branch of Planned Parenthood (though now organizationally separate), conceded that "fifty-four percent of women having abortions [in 2000 and 2001] used a contraceptive method during the month they became pregnant."[40]

Planned Parenthood markets more than just condoms and abortions. It produces a wide variety of products, including bracelets, beach balls, T-shirts, tote bags, calendars, coffee mugs, chocolates, baby hats, baby jumpers (onesies), booklets, pins, posters, "Choice on Earth" Christmas cards, and more.

One such product offered online is a package of multi-colored six-inch rulers that read, "Does Size Matter?"[41] The sexual innuendo is palpable. In fact, the ruler actually directs people to visit the sexually debauched Teenwire.com.

Another product marketed by America's leading abortion provider was a T-shirt, which simply reads, "I had an Abortion." Planned Parenthood sold the shirt for $15, claiming that post-abortive women could "assert a powerful message in support of women's rights."[42]

Abortion versus Adoption

I cannot understand how Planned Parenthood spokespeople manage to keep a straight face while claiming that the organization wants to reduce the annual number of abortions. Its own reported trends suggest that it is far more interested in recording profits. Between 1997 and 2003, the number of annual abortions in America has dropped by all accounts. Meanwhile, the annual number of abortions performed in Planned Parenthood clinics has risen 48 percent—increasing with each passing year. At the same time, Planned Parenthood's annual adoption referrals have plummeted 81 percent (see diagram 5).[43]

YEAR	ABORTIONS VS.	ADOPTION REFERRALS
2003:	244,628	1,774
2002:	227,375	1,963
2001:	213,026	1,951
2000:	197,070	2,486
1999:	182,792	2,999
1998:	168,509	4,892
1997:	165,174	9,381

diagram 5

This trend confirms Planned Parenthood's agenda!

Black Genocide

Few people would deny that Planned Parenthood founder Margaret Sanger's ambitions in launching the birth control movement hinged on her biases regarding race and class. Sanger, herself, would later write, "I hated the wretchedness and hopelessness of the poor, and never experienced that satisfaction in working among them that so many noble women have found."[44]

Only two decades before Hitler launched his plans to create the perfect race, Margaret Sanger had published several articles in the *Birth Control Review* demonstrating a morbid interest in eugenics (attempting to improve the human race through selective breeding).

On January 20, 1992, *Citizen* Magazine published an article pointing out Sanger's fascination with eugenics. The article read, "While Planned Parenthood's current apologists try to place some distance between the eugenics and birth control movements, history definitively says otherwise."

Sanger wrote articles with titles like "Some Moral Aspects of Eugenics" (June 1920); "The Eugenic Conscience" (February 1921); "The Purpose of Eugenics" (December 1924); "Birth Control and Positive Eugenics" (July 1925); and "Birth Control: The True Eugenics" (August 1928).[45]

When Sanger opened her first clinic, it was staffed by a black physician and a black social worker in a poor section of Harlem. Later, when African-American activists began to voice concerns about the purpose of Sanger's birth control clinics, she wrote her colleague, Dr. Clarence J. Gamble, stating:

> ...if we can train the Negro doctor at the clinic, he can go among them with enthusiasm and with knowledge, which, I believe, will have far-reaching results... His work, in my opinion, should be entirely with the Negro profession and the nurses, hospital, social workers, as well as the county's white doctors. His success will depend upon his personality and his training by us.
>
> The minister's work is also important, and also he should be trained, perhaps by the Federation, as to our ideals and the goal that we hope to reach. We do not want word to go out that we want to exterminate the Negro population, and the minister is the man who can straighten out that idea if it ever occurs.[46]

Many people claim this quote is taken out of context and actually that it should be taken to reflect Sanger's concern for accurately communicating her true desire to aid and assist the African-American community. I can only say that you can draw your own conclusions in the context of her well-documented agenda.

The truth is that the legacy of Planned Parenthood continues to haunt the African-American community, as abortion has now become the leading cause of death for black Americans—an average of 1,452 deaths per day. Unquestionably, the abortion industry targets the poorer African-American communities, and though blacks comprise only 12 percent of the U.S. population, black women account for 32 percent of abortions! A study conducted by the Centers for Disease Control documented that "the abortion rate for black women was 3.1 times the rate for white women."[47]

Renowned author Michael Novak points out the devastating effect that this has had on the African-American community: "Without abortion, America's black community would now number 41 million persons. It would be 35 percent larger than it is. Abortion has swept through the black community like a scythe, cutting down every fourth member."

Strange Bedfellows

This brings to light the rather puzzling relationship between Planned Parenthood, politics and the African-American community. This strange relationship is illustrated by the comments of Senator John Kerry during his 2004 presidential campaign. Democrats have for years enjoyed the support of the African American voting block, despite the party's strong support for abortion. John Kerry toed that party line and made it clear on numerous occasions that he supports abortion. Naturally, it produced great anxiety and confusion among Kerry supporters when he proclaimed on ABC News that he also believes life begins at conception. Additionally, he had made similarly confusing statements in Iowa, when appealing to a largely Catholic-based community. Asked to explain the apparent contradiction between these quasi pro-life comments and his well-known and public support of abortion, he gave a classic Kerry answer, replete with nuance and doubletalk.

He "clarified" his statements by distinguishing human life from personhood. His position is that the unborn child is not a person, according to the law. Though human, the unborn child is not protectable human life. That means Kerry adheres to and supports the decision made in *Roe v. Wade*. And that means he undoubtedly supports abortion.

This seriously flawed notion that someone can be human but not a person is not new. It was used most infamously by the U.S. Supreme Court in 1857 to justify slavery. In the *Dred Scott* decision, the Court didn't consider whether African Americans were human. The Court ruled that African Americans simply weren't persons under the law, deserving rights and protection.

Here is exactly what the Court had to say in 1857:

> For more than a century before [the Negro has] been regarded as beings of an inferior order and altogether unfit ... they had no rights which the white man was bound to respect ... the Negro might justly and lawfully be reduced to slavery ... bought and sold and treated as an ordinary article of merchandise and traffic, whenever a profit could be made.[48]

Ironically, very few leading members of the black community see the similarities in the Kerry and Supreme Court positions—let alone the offense. To the contrary, John Kerry and the Democratic party successfully court the majority of black voters. For example, Kerry assured black churchgoers that he shares their "common future, hopes, and dreams." When Kerry took his turn on stage to speak to the members of the National Association for the Advancement of Colored People at its most recent convention, he said that the government needs to do more for African Americans to improve education, the economy, and civil rights.

The question is: how does his advocacy and love for African Americans square with his pro-abortion platform?

According to the website, www.Blackgenocide.org, more black children are killed by abortion than are born. As previously stated, in the last 30 years more than 25 percent of the black population has been aborted. That means twice as many African Americans have died from abortion than from AIDS, accidents, violent crimes, cancer, and heart disease combined. Margaret Sanger, founder of Planned Parenthood and the Negro Project, wanted to use abortion to, as www.blackgenocide.org states, "restrict—many believe exterminate—the black population."[49]

So there you have the ironic and inexplicable relationship. Kerry and the Democratic party successfully court one of the most important Democratic constituencies by promising to support and defend a scheme that targets them for death through abortion. What's worse, using the rhetoric of civil rights, Kerry and others like him defend their stand on abortion with the same arguments used by the Supreme Court of 1857 to deny black Americans their freedom.

Fortunately, there is a growing awareness among African

Americans of the genocide taking place in their communities. But a very real question remains: Why doesn't the political party that claims to represent and care most about this block of voters call for an investigation of an abortion business that appears to target its base of support for annihilation? To the contrary, Congress continues to advance the Margaret Sanger agenda with our tax dollars!

The Abortion Breast Cancer Link

Another hard to explain partnership requires a look at the debate over the link between abortion and breast cancer. A recent study announced that a natural pregnancy hormone, human chorionic gonadotropin, shows promise for preventing breast cancer. According to researchers, this hormone activates tumor-suppressor genes that stop cancer cell growth. This affirms for some and suggests to many that the unnatural termination of a pregnancy with its commensurate effects on hormone levels, (such as HCG), actually increases the risk of breast cancer.

Supporting just such a link between abortion and breast cancer are groups like the Coalition on Abortion/Breast Cancer. They cite reports dating back to 1986 in which "government scientists wrote a letter to the British journal *The Lancet* acknowledging that induced abortion before the first term pregnancy increases the risk of breast cancer."[50]

They also cite a 2001 report in the *Journal of the National Cancer Institute*, which indicates a 40 percent increase in the cases of breast cancer among women in the generation following *Roe v. Wade*.[51] They further report on their website, ww.abortionbreastcancer.com, that as of 2005, "seven medical groups say abortion is one of the causes of the disease."

By stark contrast, Planned Parenthood, the nation's leading abortion provider, slams the theory as blatantly false. According to Dr. Vanessa Cullins, vice president for medical affairs at Planned Parenthood Federation of America, "There is no truth to this [theory] at all. It is one of those nasty myths invented by anti-choice organizations to frighten women away from having an abortion."[52]

Stuck in the middle of this debate is the Susan G. Komen Foundation. This is the foundation that uses events such as the famous "Race for the Cure" to raise money to fight breast cancer. According to its website, the Komen Foundation works "through a network of U.S. and international affiliates ... to eradicate breast cancer as a life-threatening disease by funding research grants and supporting education, screening and treatment projects in communities around the world."[53]

The problem is that the Komen Foundation uses some of its funds to support Planned Parenthood. This raises the question as to whether the Komen Foundation has literally struck a deal with the devil. It also creates a possible dilemma for pro-lifers who support breast cancer research through the Komen Foundation.

The fact is that local chapters of the Komen Foundation supplied nearly half a million dollars in grants to local Planned Parenthood affiliates in 2003. They have also continued to fund Planned Parenthood in 2004, with plans for continued support in 2005.

When complaints began to emerge a few years back about funding Planned Parenthood, the Komen Foundation defiantly circled the wagons by announcing their resolve to continue funding the abortion performer.

The question is that if it is even *possible* that abortions are linked to increased risk of breast cancer, what could be the logic for

Komen's support of Planned Parenthood?

There is simply no illness that touches our lives and hearts like breast cancer. Having battled another form of cancer, I find few women more inspiring than those who have beaten the illness. So I am incensed at the relationship between the Komen Foundation and Planned Parenthood.

Abortion kills. Thanks to advances in technology, like the human genome project and 4D ultrasound, everyone knows that abortion ends the life of an unborn baby. There is also a strong case to be made that abortion kills the spirit of women who have them, whether consciously or subconsciously. The plain question before us is whether it is also taking the life of women physically through breast cancer.

Surely it is time we put politics aside and get at the truth of abortion, its effects, and its relationship to breast cancer. Or shall we close our eyes to the chilling possibility that abortion providers take the life of children in one room while holding out hope for life through breast cancer education, treatment, and screening in the next?

Regardless of the answers, who in good conscience would support the Komen Foundation? This is a difficult question, because we all know someone battling breast cancer, if not running in the Komen Foundation's "Race for the Cure." I for one cannot support life and death at the same time by funneling money to Planned Parenthood. I would rather donate my dollars directly to local cancer research facilities.

In summation, we need to stop the direct and indirect funding of Planned Parenthood, which is in the morally bankrupt business of killing children in the womb by using taxpayer dollars. The American people must demand that Congress pass legislation to make better use of our collective tax dollars—and discontinue all funding of America's leading performer of abortion and purveyor of sexual anarchy.

This brings us to a place of action in the war against abortion. We obviously need to change the law to protect the unborn, but legislative action is only one of three major fronts in the abortion battle. The other two are judicial activism and medical technology. Let's take a closer look at these three major battlegrounds in the war over abortion.

Chapter 4

Theaters of War

There are three key fronts in the national abortion conflict: legislatures, courts, and medical technology. This list might seem to some like a no-brainer, but each front must be discussed to determine how to effectively fight for and win back a pro-life culture in America. Let's begin with the legislatures.

Legislatures

The frontline of legislative action requires encouraging passage of appropriate measures, discouraging inappropriate bills, and remaining informed at all times of all pending pro-life or pro-abortion legislation—both at the state and federal levels. The American people must demand that Congress make better use of our collective tax dollars—and discontinue all funding of America's leading performer of abortion and purveyor of sexual anarchy.

In various states throughout the nation, lawmakers have proposed legislation to prohibit the flow of tax dollars to abortion performers. For instance, in 2003 the Texas legislature passed an appropriations bill reserving federal tax dollars exclusively for healthcare providers that *do not* offer abortion services. Immediately, six Planned Parenthood affiliates filed a federal lawsuit claiming that such exclusivity was unconstitutional. Not surprisingly, they found a sympathetic federal judge who issued an injunction against the provision and restored Planned Parenthood's funding. However, in March 2005, the 5th U.S. Circuit Court of Appeals ruled that the Texas legislature was within its constitutional rights to withhold federal funding from abortion performers.[54]

Less than six months later, after Texas officials had shifted $2.5 million to crisis pregnancy centers, Planned Parenthood announced plans to shut down its clinic in Pharr, Texas—citing a $200,000 funding cut to its Hidalgo County chapter. Claudia Stravato, chief executive officer of Planned Parenthood of Amarillo and the Texas Panhandle, told reporters that one clinic was closed due to insufficient government funding to reimburse the organization. In an interview with the *Amarillo Globe-News*, she commented on yet another closing, saying, "We are basically in survival mode here. Nobody wants to close clinics and cut services, but we can only do so much with so little."[55]

This is, of course, an example of what can happen and what is happening at the state level in the area of legislative activity. At the federal level there are always bills of concern to the pro-life debate.

At the time of this writing some examples include the following.

1. Child Interstate Abortion Notification Act (CIANA) H.R.748 / Child Custody Protection Act (CPPA) S.403. This bill criminalizes the transportation of minors across state lines to obtain an abortion in circumvention of state laws.

2. Unborn Child Pain Awareness Act H.R. 356 / S.51. This bill requires any abortionist to provide specified information to any woman seeking an abortion at 20 weeks or later, regarding the pain that would be inflicted on the baby and to obtain a signed form accepting or rejecting administration of pain-relieving drugs to the baby.

3. Public Health Service Act—Embryonic Stem Cell Research H.R.810 / S.471. This bill provides federal funds for stem cell research that requires the killing of human embryos.

4. Cloning Prohibition Act H.R.1357 / S.658. This bill prohibits the creation of human embryos by cloning for any purpose. Unfortunately, legislators have failed to pass any such legislation for more than four years. As you might expect, in the absence of federal legislation on human cloning, fourteen states have enacted their own laws. Currently, seven permit or encourage human cloning research with state funding, including California, New Jersey, and Connecticut. More states are expected to pass permissive cloning laws. This is largely in response to the

pressure to compete in this technology market and attract top-level researchers to state universities, technology corporations, and medical facilities.

Laws like these will affect each and every one of us. For example, Governor Arnold Schwarzenegger of California was recently quoted as saying he would kill anyone who took his minor daughter across state lines for an abortion. That speaks directly to the Child Interstate Abortion Notification Act. If you think legislation like this isn't important, ask yourself what you would do if someone took your daughter across state lines for an abortion without your knowledge.

Naturally, the details and specific legislation at both the state and federal levels will be ever changing. These examples are intended to illustrate the impact both good and bad legislation can have on the pro-life debate, as well as the importance of staying vigilant in this ongoing battleground over abortion.

We cannot afford to let pro-abortion legislation move forward at either the state or federal level. It is incumbent on all those who recognize the inherent value of life to stay educated on legislation that would either hurt or advance the cause of the unborn. That means we must also be willing to put pressure on our elected representatives to vote in accordance with our beliefs on these issues.

The Courts

The second national battleground most influencing the war on abortion is the courts. Few can deny that for more than 50 years Americans have watched powerlessly as judicial activists have created public policy by the swing of a gavel. Gone are the days when moral issues were determined by the majority through their elected representatives.

The courts have, on repeated occasions, usurped the role of the legislature, so that control of the court has become tantamount to control of the nation. This explains the vicious fight in approving judicial nominees, best exemplified in the 1987 Judge Bork hearings. The impact of a single Supreme Court judge is staggering and ultimately felt by every American.

Consider, for example, what I call the "Supreme Court Swing," a short list of decisions *where conservatives lost by only one vote.*

> *Lee v. Weisman*—Banned prayer at graduations (1992)
>
> *Planned Parenthood v. Casey*—Upheld *Roe v. Wade* (1992)
>
> *Stenberg v. Carhart*—Overturned partial birth abortion ban (2000)
>
> *Grutter v. Bollinger*—Upheld affirmative action in university admissions policies (2003)
>
> *McCreary County v. ACLU of Kentucky*—Banned public displays of Ten Commandments (2005)

Decisions like these reveal that by a single vote, the course of our nation can be determined. What is worse is the sheer volume of decisions made in the last 50 or so years that demonstrate a clear departure from traditional Judeo-Christian values. Consider the following decisions made by the courts—once again not by our duly elected representatives.

> *Everson v. Board of Education*—Created separation of church and state (1947)
>
> *Engle v. Vitale*—Outlawed prayer in school (1962)
>
> *Abington v. Schempp*—Barred Bible reading in

school (1963)

Roe v. Wade—Legalized abortion-on-demand (1973)

Stone v. Graham—Banned Ten Commandments displays at school (1980)

Allegheny v. ACLU—Outlawed public nativity scenes (1989)

Ashcroft v. Free Speech Coalition—Overturned child pornography laws (2002)

Lawrence v. Texas—Established a right to sodomy (2003)

Locke v. Davey—Revoked state-funded scholarships for theology majors (2004)

Kelo v. New London—Allowed government to trample property rights (2005)

Liberal judges legislating from the bench are *creating* law instead of interpreting it. Many recognize that the placement of liberals on the bench is a deliberate and well-executed strategy of the left. Of course, the far left does not represent mainstream America. They are *not* in the majority. What better way, then, to advance a marginal view and agenda than by usurping the role of the people by legislating from the bench?

It is important to recognize that this is not just a concern for Supreme Court nominees. Rather, judicial advancement of the liberal agenda is taking place across America. That makes local politicians and law enforcement leaders critically important. Concern and awareness should begin with whomever holds the power to put lawyers on the bench at the local level. No one can afford to wait exclusively for the big fights taking place over a seat on the federal bench. Most judges begin their careers on a local bench.

What happens if we don't watch and attempt to influence local appointments? Well, the groundwork for a runaway judiciary that will ultimately make itself arbiter of all life and death decisions is not so hard to imagine. Does that sound hysterical to you? What of Terri Schiavo? Or consider the following true story from across the pond.

A beautiful 22 month-old baby girl (at the time of this writing) named Charlotte Wyatt is terribly ill. Born prematurely at 26 weeks, she has serious heart and lung problems. She has never left the hospital and is fed through a tube.

In the span of her very short life, she has stopped breathing three times. Each time she was resuscitated. However, doctors at the treating hospital in England do not want to revive her should her breathing fail a fourth time.

They say keeping her alive is futile and causes suffering. Her parents strongly disagree. They believe Charlotte, who is responsive to them, is not suffering. Their hope is that maybe she will live long enough and become strong enough to one day walk outside and see the sky and the trees.

Due to the parent's conflict with the attending physicians and the hospital, the dispute went before the British High Court where the judge sided with the doctors and hospital. The court agreed with the medical professionals who argued that Charlotte's poor quality of life disqualified her from further treatment. This means that that should Charlotte enter into crisis again, she would not receive necessary care, but be left to die. Fortunately, that decision was recently overturned by the British High Court and on December 7, 2005 Charlotte Wyatt was taken home for the very first time.[56]

Unfortunately, the fight faced by Charlotte's parents represents a worldwide trend toward the well-established path laid by the Dutch Parliament decades ago when it legalized euthanasia. Let me explain: As originally defined, euthanasia was limited in scope to taking the life of a terminally ill patient at the patient's expressed request.

The main argument for euthanasia in the Netherlands and everywhere has always been the need for more patient autonomy. Advocates assert patient rights, including the right to make their own end-of-life decisions. Yet, over the past 20 years, Dutch euthanasia practice has ultimately given doctors, not patients, the deciding vote on who should live or die.

According to the first official government study on the practice of euthanasia in the Netherlands in 1990, 1,040 people (an average of three per day) were actively killed by doctors without the patients' knowledge or consent.[57] Since then, the killing of non-consenting adults has been on the rise and has expanded to include competent people with incurable illnesses or disabilities; patients who are not physically ill, but depressed, and desire to commit suicide; and incompetent people with an illness such as Alzheimer's.

In addition to the rise in killing adults without their consent or knowledge, it is now standard practice in the Netherlands to withhold treatment from premature or disabled children, as well as to euthanize seriously ill children under the age of 12. The British medical journal *Lancet* reported in 1997 that Dutch doctors are killing approximately eight percent of all infants who die each year.[58] A fifth of these killings is done without the consent of the parents. Of course, all occurred without the consent of the children.

Doctors in the Netherlands are also renowned for withholding treatment from psychiatric patients and the elderly. It is no secret that the elderly often avoid hospitalization for fear they will be put to death. They reportedly wear arm bracelets instructing doctors to not take their lives or they go to nursing facilities in Germany where euthanasia is illegal.[59]

The most frequent reasons given by Dutch doctors for ending

the lives of patients without their knowledge or consent are low quality of life and no prospect for improvement. This is the very reason now given in England for withholding treatment from Charlotte Wyatt.

However, all of this is taking place an ocean away, right? What can it possibly mean to us here at home in the U.S.? Well let's see.

1. We kill thousands of children every day in America through abortion, some by the most brutal methods and only moments before they are born.

2. Hundreds of thousands of unborn children kept in frozen storage are now targeted for sacrifice and human experimentation by proponents of stem cell research.

3. The American Medical Association wrote an opinion that has since been withdrawn for further study, stating that severely disabled children born with anencephaly should have their organs harvested for transplant, even before they die.[60]

4. The Supreme Court of Florida ruled that Terri Schiavo should be starved to death, based largely on the misdiagnosis that she was unaware of her surroundings and unable to feel or interact with those around her.[61]

5. We have legalized physician-assisted suicide in Oregon, with attempts to pass similar legislation in California and Washington.

Based on these current trends, and the well-executed strategy to advance the liberal agenda through judicial activism, I expect to see more and more life-and-death decisions like that concerning Charlotte Wyatt coming to a courtroom near home in the foreseeable future. That is, unless the sleeping giant in America (the millions of self-identified Christians who have disengaged from the political and cultural warfare in our midst) wake up to fight against this tidal surge of pro-death sentiment now overtaking America.

Medical Technology

Adding to the somewhat predictable trend of liberal judges legislating from the bench is the somewhat unpredictable impact of advances in medical technology. This third frontline fight is, unbeknownst to most people, almost always a repackaging of the abortion debate. The reason most people don't recognize it as such is that it is often cloaked by technical terms and procedures. This is often a deliberate attempt to insure that those who might object to these technologies are not informed and aroused.

The current flashpoint along the medical technology frontline is the use of embryonic stem cells in search of cures. Stem cells are the basic building blocks for all the tissues of the body. Researchers hope to treat human diseases by using stem cells taken from embryos. In August of 2001 President Bush announced federal dollars could be used to fund research on existing stem cell lines, because the embryos were already destroyed. He drew the line in the sand by saying that *no additional embryos* would be destroyed for stem cell research using our tax dollars.

After 20 years of research, embryonic stem cells have not cured a single lab rat. They have not been used to treat people because the cells are unproven and unsafe. They tend to produce tumors, cause transplant rejection, and form the wrong kinds of cells. Worst of all, human lives are sacrificed to obtain embryonic stem cells.

So even if the pie-in-the-sky cures that proponents espouse were actually attainable, pursuit of this technology would be wrong. It is morally reprehensible that we would sacrifice the unborn for advances in medicine, no matter how we are tempted. That said, the pursuit of this technology is particularly egregious because ethical alternatives exist.

At the time of this writing, adult stem cells have treated over 65 diseases in human patients in published clinical studies.[62] This number will no doubt increase. In the treatment using adult stem cells, no lives are sacrificed. Generally the adult stem cells are isolated from the very patient needing treatment. Some of the most startling advances have come in treating blood disorders, juvenile diabetes, and spinal cord injuries.

For example, right here in America, three young women, Laura Dominguez, Susan Fajt, and Melissa Holley, who all suffered paralysis resulting from spinal cord injuries, regained muscle control, thanks to a procedure using adult stem cells taken from their own noses. Incredibly, Dominguez and Fajt are now walking with assistance. Holley has so far regained bladder control and arm and leg movement. Additionally, umbilical cord blood cells were used in South Korea to treat a woman who had been paralyzed for 19 years. She can now walk with braces.[63]

Regarding the treatment of diabetes, Dr. Denise Faustman, a leading diabetes researcher from Harvard, has completely reversed end-stage juvenile diabetes in mice and has FDA approval to begin a human clinical trial.[64] Additionally, a team of doctors in Argentina has successfully pioneered a technique that involves the injection of adult stem cells into patients with Type 2 diabetes to restore pancreatic function. By contrast, the journal *Diabetologia* reported failure in trying to get embryonic stem cells to treat diabetes. Instead the embryo cells formed tumors in the mice.[65]

This may beg the question "Why the embryonic stem cell

research hype?" The answer in this case is that big biotech is driven by money. They want patentable discoveries that will make them rich. Scientists also want to strike gold. That often means conducting research unfettered by ethical constraints. Lastly, abortionists don't want to lose any political ground, and that demands that the unborn remain an expendable commodity. As a result, these groups are combining their efforts to advance embryonic stem cell research in order to advance their individual goals.

The take-home message regarding this technology is that embryonic stem cell research is unsafe, unethical, unproven, and unnecessary in light of advances using adult stem cells. More generally speaking, federal funding should never be used to pay for research that many Americans know is morally wrong.

We must, however, keep in mind that embryonic stem cell research is only the most current and pressing issue in medical technology. Another controversy closely related to embryonic stem cell research is human cloning. Just 25 years ago the debate was over fetal tissue research. Naturally, it is difficult to guess what will come next, but a sharp eye will see the repackaging of the abortion debate about the sanctity of human life every time.

We need to be aware of the arguments made by proponents of such unethical technologies. It is always the same. "The technology will help and is necessary to alleviate someone's suffering." This is a very seductive and impassioned argument. So we must be vigilant in properly phrasing the real question to emphasize what is really at stake. In other words, who among us would want a cure if you understood it meant the sacrifice of another's life without that person's consent? Of course, this may seem an easy question to answer, if you are not currently in need of a life-saving cure or near miraculous advance in medicine. So out of a sense of fairness and proper context, I talked with a friend of mine who is paralyzed from the waist down to get his opinion on the research and hope offered by embryonic stem cell research.

Paralyzed and Opposed

His name is Will York, and he has been my husband's best friend since childhood. He is 6 feet, 5 inches tall, blonde, broad shouldered, with a chiseled chin and infectious smile. All those handsome physical features aside, the real story of Will York is deep beneath the surface.

Not long after meeting Will, I discovered he ran marathons. He took the ROTC class in college and went through Ranger training, "just for the fun of it." Will delighted in snow-laden camping trips, paddled through the Amazon, climbed mountains, skied the great slopes of Colorado, and biked across Alaska.

Bitten by the acting bug and a call to fame, he went west to Hollywood. Many producers called him the "hardest working person" out there. Knowing Will, he tried to live up to that description every moment of every day.

I wasn't sure what to expect when he left for L.A., but I wouldn't have been surprised to see him become the latest heartthrob in daytime television, sell aftershave, or make his TV debut on *Survivor*.

Sadly, all my expectations changed, as did his, one fall day in 2001. I got a phone call while working at home that sent me to my knees in prayer. Will had been in a serious mountain biking accident; the prognosis was very bad.

I would learn later that 10 minutes before the accident, Will was on top of a mountain enjoying the itching and twitching of his legs that often come after a two-hour up-hill ride (not as if I would know). He was one of those fitness freaks who was looking forward to being sore the next day. Ironically, the ride had been challenging enough that it made him pause and thank God for his legs and the ability to ride.

A few minutes later, Will went over a hidden and sudden 12-foot drop into a ditch. To avoid landing on his face, he did a front flip and landed on his back. The sudden pain of multiple broken ribs and vertebra was the most intense pain he had ever known. The pain was immediately followed by the terror of realizing he couldn't feel or move his legs. In that very moment, he remembers chanting, "Please God, don't let me be paralyzed. I want to learn to tap dance." That prayer has so far gone unanswered.

It has been four years since Will became paralyzed from the waist down. He has been largely confined to a wheel chair, struggling daily with continuing pain. He has faced multiple surgeries and intense therapies. The greatest challenge of all has been learning how to live life all over again from a seated position.

Admittedly, we all wondered in the early days after the accident how it might change him. Today, few are surprised that he has the courage and strength to conquer the challenges paralysis brought into his life. In part, we are humbled as we secretly wonder if we would have or could have done as well. He is a living testament to an unquenchable human spirit. He is also an inspiration to those seeking the strength that comes from a life deeply rooted in faith and a relationship with Jesus Christ.

He remains in California, where he has made a new life for himself, complete with the occasional skiing trip (although from a chair). He now talks of returning to school to pursue a life in apologetics.

Will says this is a different kind of "roughing it" than hiking in the Amazon or biking in Alaska, but living through it is similarly rewarding.

As for a cure, Will prays that God will bless the scientists who are searching. He remains ever hopeful of restored function to his legs and lower body. But he also prays that no one will ever use his injury and condition as an excuse to kill someone else, which is exactly the case with embryonic stem cell research. He says he would rather be in his wheelchair for the rest of his life than sacrifice an innocent life so that he might run again.

He still thanks God for his legs, but is more thankful for his life. His greatest hope is that the sanctity of human life will always be honored above his comfort—and even a cure. Will understands like few people ever will that for the unborn to one day enjoy for themselves legs that work and "roughing it" in the wild, they must first be allowed to live.

Creating Peter to Save Paul

Embryonic stem cell research is technology that may seem far removed from everyday life. But is it really? Consider another current trend related to embryonic stem cell research, one that requires the sacrifice of the unborn. This practice is called pre-implantation genetic diagnosis. It takes place when a sibling is needed to save the life of an already existing child. The problem is that the needed sibling does not yet exist. Consider this hypothetical plea from a mother eager to save the life of her child.

> *Is it wrong to create a baby that might hold a cure for my dying son?*
>
> *Before you decide, let me say that Aaron was born only after I lost three other children by miscarriage. So he is my world; bringing light and love and laughter into my every day. When he hurts, I suffer with him in every breath.*

When his frail body gives way under the grip of illness, I think, "Why can't it be me?" Like so many mothers, I would give my life for him.

When I first understood he was sick and needed a bone-marrow transplant, we tested everyone in the family to determine compatibility between our tissue and his. There was no match. Then after exhausting every available medical treatment with no results, I heard of a treatment called pre-implantation genetic diagnosis.

The technique, being used in Chicago, can test embryos for a tissue type match. So using in-vitro fertilization, my husband and I created 15 tiny lives and had them tested. Only one was a healthy match, so we implanted that embryo and gave the others away for research.

We brought our second son to full term, naming him Adam. Almost immediately we used the stem cells from the umbilical cord for treating Aaron. Miraculously, the stem cells saved Aaron's life. We are now a very happy family of four. My sons are both healthy at 5 and 2, thanks to God and modern medicine.

Such might be the testimony of any of the nine desperate couples with children needing bone-marrow transplants, who created designer babies with the help of the Reproductive Genetics Institute in Chicago. They announced that five children were recently born in the hope that their stem cells could provide a cure for their siblings who are suffering with blood disease.

The question: "Is it wrong?"

These are the kinds of real-life and every-day dilemmas we face in the twenty-first century. It is a century of very fast-paced technology—moving faster, in fact, than most people can absorb. So if we can't keep pace with the technology, how can we keep up with the entanglement of ethical and moral ramifications that come with it? We must admit if we don't adequately understand the technology or the associated moral implications, we are ill-equipped to make sound judgments on its use.

In situations like these, however difficult, we cannot be too shortsighted to see that to condone or agree with the choice of one or even nine desperate mothers gives way to a utilitarian mindset. That is a mindset that can and does ultimately lead a people to condone or even accept as "right" situations where some members of society become "sacrificial lambs" to serve the interests of the majority. Obviously, taken to its logical end, segments of society will be continually targeted for sacrifice when they are deemed to be "of better use dead than alive."

Today, it is the unborn through stem cell research and various IVF procedures that are selected and sacrificed, based on genetic makeup. Even worse, there is a law in New Jersey that allows children born through a human cloning procedure to be killed—even after they are born.

If we allow this mindset to take further hold of our nation, who will be next—the mentally disabled, the physically disabled, the elderly? What happens if you become part of the next group targeted? Who will defend you and on what grounds?

It cannot be overlooked that despite the success of the treatment and the medical justification, the fact remains that our hypothetical Adam was conceived, not just to be a son, but a medical treatment. Adam was a means—valuable only insofar as he carried the right genetic material. If he hadn't, he would have been rejected and sacrificed to research just like his other 14 embryonic siblings.

In considering advancing medical technologies, such as embryonic stem cell research, the obvious question is whether the sacrifice of innocent life should ever be condoned, even if it is intended to advance the noblest of ends.

Yet it is easy to see from these examples how medical technology can complicate the abortion debate. Unfortunately, few people genuinely understand the details behind such technologies, and when desperate for a cure, they often choose not to focus on what might stand in the way of their cure. This all points to the need to conduct and advance medicine within ethical boundaries and avoid placing people in the horrible position that the hypothetical scenario creates.

What technology will come next to seduce the public into longer life and better health? No one can be certain. What is certain is that without a clear foundation in traditional and fundamental life values, our nation is destined for a path of corruption in pursuit of twenty-first century medical technologies.

Chapter 5

The Way to Win

U nderstanding the three battlegrounds of legislative action, judicial activism, and medical technology that comprise the key landscape for the pro-life movement raises the question, "How can we make a difference to, dare I say, win this war?" The answer is both simple and overwhelming. It begins by winning the pro-life debate in your own backyard. Each of us must be able to wrestle to the ground the often unwieldy, convoluted, and complicated shell game of arguments, word games, and unworkable philosophies that our opponents are so adept at using. Only from there can we set a grassroots prairie fire capable of sweeping the nation. In other words, win in your backyard, and we can win the nation. It begins with you right here, right now.

With that in mind, I propose a strategy for tackling all aspects of the pro-life debate with a simple campaign based on L.I.F.E. So let's go.

Legislate Morality

"L" stands for legislate. That is, legislate our own brand of morality. We have already seen firsthand how the right legislation can put a financial hurt on Planned Parenthood in Texas and other states across the nation. But to put Planned Parenthood out of business permanently, we need to overcome a psychological battle when it comes to the issue of abortion and legislation. That is, we must rebuff the nonsense argument that "we don't legislate morality in this nation." To the contrary, every law is someone's idea of what is right or wrong. The very purpose of the law is to restrain and punish heartless and depraved behavior.

Of course, one very common response to the subject of rules and the rule of law is—"Who needs 'em?" In fact, many share the famous line from Shakespeare's *Henry VI.* That is, "The first thing we do, let's kill all the lawyers." Its meaning is intended to convey at least one madman's idea of nirvana. Of course, most people living beyond a frat party mentality recognize that it falsely implies that a world with no rules, or at least no one to defend them, is the greatest place to live. Want proof that this is nonsense outside the abortion debate? How about the debacle at Abu Ghraib prison?

Here existed a world within the war where the rules were temporarily suspended. The result was not nirvana. What may have started with all the appearances of a frat party eventually spiraled out of control. When order did emerge, the only ones enjoying themselves were those who came into power by brute force, fear, and intimidation. This is the environment that led to the human rights violations that for a time totally preoccupied our media, armed forces, and critics of American culture worldwide.

So the need for rules and adherence to them is obvious. They are a necessary part of a civilized society. First, to protect ourselves we need to know the rules in any given circumstance. Next, we need to understand that adherence to the rules is what ensures, at least in America, equal treatment and equal freedoms, especially for the weakest and most vulnerable in our society. Finally, rules build in people a sense of security and stability, providing boundaries and safe limits of conduct. They even provide a sense of fair play in war, as given by the Geneva Conventions.

So how does this apply to the current subject matter of abortion? It is actually quite simple. In this society we are willing to criminalize all kinds of corrupt activity, such as rape, theft, arson, and murder. It logically follows that since abortion is most often the deliberate taking of a life, it is murder and should be legislated against with "no apologies and no exceptions."

Too many people mistakenly think that abortion is exclusively an issue of the heart and that the Church only needs to work harder through prayer. They are wrong. Martin Luther King, Jr. once said (and I paraphrase) that he "couldn't make men love him but [he] could keep them from lynching him." That was by changing the law.

Of course, it is naturally and necessarily incumbent on the Church to pray for hearts to change, but prayer alone is simply not enough. No one would stand by silently praying as a child was being raped before one's very eyes. Why do we stand by silently while more than 3,500 children are being murdered every day?

One answer is that the evil of abortion is a stealth enterprise. It is kept in the dark, behind the closed doors of abortion clinics, doctor's offices, and laboratories. The records of failed or botched abortions as well as those performed on rape victims, minors, and those without informed consent are well-hidden with all the other abortion records by doctor-patient confidentiality laws. So what do we do?

We need to start legislating our own brand of morality, beginning at the local level. What is working in places across America is the passing of legislation, such as the previously discussed restriction on taxpayer dollars. Other successfully passed legislation includes parental notification, informed consent, and one-to-five day cooldown laws. We also need to criminalize harm to the unborn. This has been accomplished to some degree at the federal level; it needs to happen in every state and locality.

Adoption laws are another possible target for legislative action. There is a mantra that says abortion needs to remain legal as long as our adoption houses are full of unwanted babies. However, according to the National Council for Adoption, this isn't true. There is no gap between birth and adoption for U.S. babies. They are adopted as soon as the paperwork is done.[66]

Mark Crutcher, founder and president of Life Dynamics, outlines the situation well in his book *On Message—Understanding and Communicating the Pro-life Position*.[67] He states that the problem is not in placing newborns, but rather the older children who come into the system long after their birth and often through foster care. That means the pool of children available for adoption has nothing to do with abortion. That further means that the children abortionists want to kill are the ones who are easiest to place for adoption. Killing an unrelated group of children, the unborn, because older children are hard to place for adoption, is nonsensical.

As for placing the older children currently living in our adoption facilities, we need to overhaul the entire placement system. The plain fact is that adoption is not an attractive option, or even a possibility, for many American families with an average income who would be willing to provide a family and home. It is simply too expensive and too entangled in red tape. What is worse is that, according to Crutcher, "The current system is costing taxpayers billions, while depriving good parents of children and doing irreparable harm to kids who have grown up without a family."

Bottom line, we need to give good families easier access to older children who need a good home. We need to simultaneously dispel the lie that aborting babies is a solution to this current problem.

Another piece of legislation that the pro-life community could advance is an "Abortion Non-discrimination Act." That is legislation that demands that "no baby can be deprived of its right to life because of its gender, race, or disability." Legislation like this could potentially bring together liberal women's groups, civil rights, and disabled advocacy groups. Imagine what more noble cause could unite such otherwise diverse groups than an "Abortion Non-discrimination Act." It could happen. I mean, even Hillary Clinton is against killing baby girls in other countries like India and China.

On a more immediately plausible note, the pro-life movement should work to pass laws requiring ultrasounds before abortion. Let mothers see the truth of the murder they are about to commit. Make women knowingly responsible for their actions. Make them look their baby in the face before they kill him or her. Sound cruel? It is not more cruel than tearing apart a child in the womb or the physical and emotional harm women suffer as a result of the abortion procedure itself.

Pursue Child Molesters

Next, we need to encourage more state attorneys general to pursue child molesters through abortion records. This is happening in Kansas and Indiana. It needs to happen everywhere. Think about it. When a 13- or 14-year-old girl has an abortion, she has been raped. She simply does not have the capacity to give legal consent to sex. That means that whoever made her pregnant should be prosecuted as a child molester.

Why aren't more state attorneys general pursuing child molesters through abortion records? Few things upset Americans more than hearing that a child was abducted, sexually assaulted, and killed. Think for a moment about the recent and highly publicized case of nine-year-old Jessica Lunsford. The crime was committed by a registered sex offender who failed to report that he relocated, as required by law.

What's worse, this repeat offender reportedly made it no secret that he was unable to control his depraved urges. His 24 arrests spanning 30 years and his rap sheet practically guaranteed his predation would continue.[68]

Just about the same time this story aired on most evening news programs, I saw a segment on *The Oprah Winfrey Show* warning of the predatory nature of child molesters. It showed an interview with a pedophile who told of the premeditated nature of his crimes. He specifically told how he manipulated his young victims to trust him.

After the interview, Oprah herself related pieces of her own story.[69]

She was molested by an uncle when she was a young girl. It wasn't until she was in her 40s that her father asked for the details of what happened. Her response to her father and the viewing audience was that no matter what happened, she was violated by her uncle and her uncle alone "was responsible."

Oprah said (and I paraphrase), "Even if I approached him naked and sat on his head, he had the responsibility to tell me to go home, put my clothes on, or walk away. He was the adult, and I was the child."

I couldn't agree with Oprah more. I strongly suspect that most of the millions of women watching her program also agreed.

So the question is: "Why don't we better protect our children and more aggressively pursue sexual predators?" Answering that question also answers why there isn't broader support for state attorneys general to pursue child molesters through abortion records.

The answer, in part, is because as a society we glamorize and promote sex through every possible venue. Selling sex is a multi-billion dollar industry. It is integral to mainstream media, available through the Internet, and sold through billboards, bookstores, and supermarkets. We not only expose adults, but also our children in grade school are exposed to every form of sexuality, including information on alternative lifestyles.

We treat children as though they are capable of adult sexual relationships when they are not. Proof can be seen almost any night in prime-time television programming, which has the impact of making both victims and predators of our children.

Just last week a local prosecutor (okay, okay it was my husband, who actually is a prosecutor) told me of one of his cases in which a 14-year-old boy molested his 4-year-old cousin. While no penetration took place, the boy's goal was to ejaculate. When asked what prompted his behavior, the boy simply replied "TV"—specifically, programming he watched on HBO.

Common sense tells us that children should not be having sex with each other or adults. It should be deterred, not encouraged or condoned. Yet, as a society we promote it and then bash those who attempt to shield or protect our children from such abuses.

Pornography, X-rated television programming, and Hollywood films are all protected through a distorted exercise of free speech and the First Amendment. Now sexual predators are, ironically, being protected through the right of privacy—the same grounds used by the Supreme Court in 1973 when discovering a constitutional right to abortion.

Standing against this tide of exposing and inundating our children with sex are Attorneys General Phill Kline of Kansas and Steve Carter of Indiana, who obviously recognize their duty to investigate such criminal activity to protect the children of their respective states. They also recognize their duty to expose and prosecute those who routinely cover up such crimes.

As you might expect, Planned Parenthood is denouncing the efforts to seize patient medical records from clinics, calling the actions "a coordinated attempt to intimidate health-care providers and patients."[70] In each case, abortion rights advocates object on grounds of privacy.

Ironically, that means the rapists go free under the veil of women's sexual freedom and right to abortion. So, instead of protecting the very people the organization supposedly exists to serve, Planned Parenthood is protecting men who abuse women and young girls.

Sadly, the reaction of Planned Parenthood isn't a surprise. The surprise is that so many millions of men and women can be alarmed and outraged by the sexual assault and murder of a 9-year-old little girl like Jessica Lunsford and not see their contribution. It lies in society's tolerance and support of abortion and sexual promiscuity in its myriad forms.

That means, in addition to quashing the over-sexualizing of our youth and protecting them against sexual predators, we also need to pass laws to push the teaching of abstinence education in school. Despite all the negative media hype, it actually does work. It is simply that peddlers of sex don't want America to believe it. The bottom line is that if we stress to kids the dangers, reality, and consequences of sex and make abortion illegal, we will see a dramatic change in the sexual activity of our children.

Truth for Lies

"I" stands for "identify and deny the lies." This section is intentionally short to demonstrate how quickly we can dispense with the often-convoluted lies of the pro-abortionist movement.

It is a simple fact that those who favor abortion never defend the act of abortion itself. Rather, they wrap the debate in a pack of convoluted and complex lies to sell abortion. They sell abortion as a privacy right, a property right, a freedom from reproduction, a necessary evil, and a solution to social ills.

To all of these lies there is a simple one-word response. The answer is "No." Abortion is not a privacy right. There is no hidden clause in the Constitution that gives the right to women to kill their children in the womb.

It is not a property right. Since the abolition of slavery, people cannot be treated as property.

It is not a reproductive freedom. I mean, let's face it; once a woman is pregnant, she already has reproduced. The only question is whether to have a live or a dead baby.

It is not a necessary evil. A mother will never have to sacrifice her life to save the life of her child. If, in saving the life of a mother, the baby's life is lost, it is tragic. However, it is not murder, as long as the intent and effort were to save both lives.

Neither is it a necessary evil in response to rape. The bottom line is that a child does not find his or her value in the circumstances of his or her conception—not even in the worst of all circumstances.

Finally, abortion is not a solution to social ills. Not a single societal problem has improved since *Roe*—not homelessness, not hunger, not child abuse.

All of these defenses of abortion are based on lies and could be written at length, but the idea is to condense the debate to its simplest terms. So all you need to remember for starters is that the answer to each of these lies begins with one word, "No!"

Free Women

"F" stands for "Free women." That is, free women from false feminism and sexual exploitation that has usurped and saturated the women's movement since the 1960s. The truth is that abortion does not empower women. However, liberals have grossly distorted feminism to be epitomized by women willing to kill their own children in the womb. To the contrary, "Real Women" don't kill their children and "Real Men" don't expect them to.

Additionally, both women and children need to be freed from sexual exploitation. Who can deny that abortion enables sexually irresponsible men to exploit women without consequences? It should come as no surprise that men, ages 18-35, are among the most ardent supporters of abortion which, by the way, poses no actual risk to men. The same cannot be said for women who undergo the horrifying procedure.

Along those lines I was encouraged by a recently released

statistic that suggests Hollywood-made movies containing explicit sex just don't sell. Based on box-office dollars, it seems that moviegoers actually prefer films with moral or Christian-based messages over the morally depraved product so frequently served up by the celebrity elite.[71] This is an unquestionable victory for traditional family values. It is not, however, an upswing in the downward-spiraling trend of an American appetite gone wild for unbridled sex of every and any kind.

It is actually a displacement—a displacement that is taking pornography off the big screen and putting it onto the little screen of our personally owned and used computers. Yes, it is closer than ever. It is right in our homes and offices through our now ever-present and instant access to the Internet.

Shocking statistics provided by the *Internet Filter Review* in 2003 claim the pornography industry is worth $57 billion worldwide— $12 billion in the U.S.[72] It is reportedly larger than the combined revenues of all professional football, baseball, and basketball franchises. Vastly accelerating this industry is Internet porn, comprising 4.2 million websites. That is 12 percent of the total number of websites with 372 million pornographic pages.

Of course, pornography has always been around. So the question is "What makes Internet pornography so powerful and insidious?"

The answer is that what once was a rather isolated problem has become a widespread crisis based on three factors uniquely related to Internet use: accessibility, affordability, and anonymity. This helps to explain why pornography is skyrocketing, even among the religious community. (It's done in secret with no hangover to hide.)

According to *Internet Filter Review* statistics, as many as 53 percent of the men who attend Promise Keepers conferences have viewed pornography. Forty-seven percent of those who define themselves as Christian admit that pornography is a major problem in the home. And while traditionally viewed as a "man's problem," Internet porn targets women too with increasing numbers of women addicted to sexually oriented chat rooms and cybersex. Worse, there are no effective age restrictions on the Internet. That means that the most susceptible among us, our children, are a prime target of both predators and purveyors.

So is this much ado about nothing? Most people publicly agree: "Porn is icky, but what people do in the privacy of their own homes is their business." With one exception, child pornography, many people defend pornography as an adult activity engaged in by consenting participants. They frequently label people who object as "religious prudes." They claim no one is getting hurt, right? Wrong.

Studies reveal that acts of sexual violence are commonly linked to pornography and the number of victims is massive. According to sworn testimony before the U.S. Senate, experts reveal that by the time a female in this country is 18 years old, 38 percent have been sexually molested. One in eight women will be raped. Fifty percent of women will be sexually harassed on their jobs during their lifetimes.[73]

So, just out of curiosity, "Where are all the defenders of women's rights?" Oh, that's right. Rather than protest the exploitation and demoralizing objectification of women, they celebrate it as an exercise of our sexual freedom and a First Amendment privilege. This, of course, is a distortion of reality. Predictably, a distorted sense of reality is a common symptom of sexual predators and addicts.

These distortions arise and are spread most commonly through none other than the pornographic media itself. Simply said, the more pornography is viewed, the more distorted one's view of sex becomes. This is called desensitization. For example, when one study group was exposed to as little as five hours of non-violent pornography, they began to think pornography was not offensive and that rapists deserved milder punishments. They also became more callous and negative toward women and developed an appetite for more deviant or violent types of pornography.

Researchers now link this change in behavior to the startling discovery that when people indulge in pornography, they release powerful chemicals that actually change the structure of the brain and body, creating a physical and chemical addiction. This is well chronicled in the book by Mark B. Kastleman, *The Drug of the New Millennium*. This addiction is so powerful, it is being likened to cocaine, alcohol, and heroin. Moreover, like any drug addiction, once hooked, addicts need harder and more perverse images to achieve the same "high."

The good news is that just like addiction to alcohol or drugs, the physical addiction to pornography can be conquered—usually through the help of an addiction recovery program. Still, the best medicine is prevention. That means accountability and installation of a complete Internet safety program consisting of an Internet filter and parental controls.

News showing that there is no big money in big-screen filmmaking that contains explicit sex is also good. That means market pressures can work for traditional family values. Therefore, we need to apply market pressure to all avenues of release for pornography, including TV, public newsstands, and the Internet.

To begin, we must come to real terms with the undeniable irony in women's "freed" sexuality. From Madonna to Britney Spears to Cat Woman, the most popular women in America and around the world are still celebrated for how well they satiate the sexual fantasies of men. But women like these have done more to set back the clock to the dark ages than any pro-life advocate. And they do it with the endorsement of NOW (National Organization for Women), NARAL Pro-Choice America, Hollywood and, naturally, Planned Parenthood.

If you are wondering about motive, the answer is tragically simple. The abortion industry makes billions of dollars from abortion as a means of birth control. They say they want women to be *free* to experience sex without any unwanted repercussions. However, such "freedom" would rarely be exercised if women understood just how badly they were being used.

Truth is, girls, almost every guy wants to date a bad girl and marry a good one. What's worse, I have never heard a woman wish, after she was married, she was more sexually permissive while she was dating—though I am sure a few exist.

Both sexual promiscuity and abortion *are sold* deceptively and subliminally. If most women knew what sexual promiscuity and abortion would cost them physically and emotionally, they would not do it. For example, according to the *British Medical Journal,* post-abortive women are six times more likely to commit suicide than women who give birth.[74] More casual sex, anyone?

Why do you think that after years of brazen exhibitionism, women like Madonna attempt to remake themselves as spirit-filled paragons of motherly virtue? I mean, is she kidding? Or do the same women who bought her bill of goods 20 years ago now buy into her current image makeover?

Why let her and her cultural progeny brainwash our young women into a lifestyle of sexual promiscuity? It is a dead end that subjects women to the control of men's sexual lusts and nothing more.

The truth is that women aren't the only ones who need to be freed from false feminism. Young girls need to be freed as well. In fact, all children and teens need to be freed from sexual exploitation and the overarching effects of a sex-crazed nation. To accomplish this goal, bold, strict, and well-educated parents are needed to protect our children.

For example, I recently stood in the cul-de-sac of my neighborhood talking to two other moms about teen sex. One of the two ladies has a 14-year-old son who raised a few red flags on the subject of sex, indicating a need to talk. This need is common among teens inundated with sex through our current cultural environment and will come as no surprise to most parents of teens today. And this is not new; it has been building for decades.

I vividly remember when I was 14. (Yes, a few decades ago.) Many girls around me had already become sexually active. By the time I entered high school—ninth grade—girls started dropping out to have babies. So, with the current cultural obsession with sex, parental intervention is needed—often before puberty.

The urgent need for education is further driven home by a recently released report on the spread of STDs (sexually-transmitted diseases) among young Americans. According to the report, an estimated 50 percent of sexually active youth (age 15-24) will contract an STD by the age of 25.

This is serious stuff. STDs include syphilis, hepatitis, gonorrhea, chlamydia, genital warts, genital herpes, trichomoniasis and HIV/AIDS. The names alone drip with yuck. Symptoms range from swelling, burning, discharge, abdominal pain, fever, fatigue, nausea, vomiting, sores, and death. What is worse, some symptoms are often recurring and lifelong—except, of course, death.

In response to the epidemic level of STD transmission, April has actually been designated National STD Awareness month. But how many of you knew that?

Public awareness surrounding the effects and problems associated with STDs is embarrassingly low—so low that according to the American Social Health Association (ASHA), there are more than 18 million new cases of STDs every year. That means at least one in four Americans will contract an STD in their lifetime.

Compounding the problem, according to ASHA, "many young people assume they are being tested for STDs during regular health visits when, in fact, such testing is not routine." That means many STD cases go undetected because some of the symptoms are mild. For example, chlamydia left untreated can cause pelvic inflammatory disease and sterility in women.

Naturally, teens should be educated on the dangers of contracting STDs and how to protect themselves. Abstinence comes immediately to mind. While generic and mild suggestions of abstinence may not work, a heaping dose of reality, complete with pictures and testimonials, might.

It is time we get honest with kids about the dangers of sex and stop pushing sex like candy. STDs can cause heart and brain damage, cancer, infertility, liver problems, blindness, deafness, and birth defects! And condoms do NOT protect against the transmission of all STDs.

Further evidence that sex education needs an overhaul is that most kids don't think oral sex is sex at all. I guess we have another reason to thank Bill Clinton. But oral sex can transmit STDs as easily and quickly as intercourse.

My hope is to see stricter parenting become a trend as a frontline defense against today's all-consuming culture of sexual promiscuity and its tentacles of consequences. I want to see it replaced with a message that respects and upholds the inherent value of all life at every stage and age, and reaffirms the unmatched reward of waiting to explore sexuality until inside the confines of a God-ordained marriage.

End the Bloodshed

The last letter in our LIFE acronym is "E," which stands for "End the bloodshed," and it is bloodshed. Science now confirms that life begins at conception. From conception we are biologically alive, genetically human, genetically and sexually distinct, and able to direct our own growth and development. It is a plain scientific fact that life is on a continuum from conception until death, whenever that occurs.

One of the most memorable debates I have had on this subject occurred at a conference where I was invited as a guest speaker on the subject of stem cell research. The conference was hosted and largely attended by conservatives in a luxury resort, complete with some very high-profile speakers, a golf tournament, and a black tie dinner.

The first evening's reception and dinner included the famed football coach Lou Holtz. I have always been a big football fan, hailing from the University of Miami and the five-time national champion Hurricanes. So as I eagerly awaited his speech, I faced the usual but nonetheless awkward hurdle of "small talk" with guests I didn't know seated at the dinner table.

I've never been a very good schmoozer. What's worse, I don't much like talking shop after business hours either. That means that despite my rather opinionated views, I usually find myself hoping someone else will take over the conversation, lest an uncomfortable silence descend upon the table, and I begin clock watching until the lead speaker takes the stage.

Fortunately, my husband attended with me (did I mention there was a golf tournament?), and he usually runs interference on dinner conversation with the agility of a seasoned politician. Unfortunately, it didn't take long for everyone to know that I was slated to speak. With such a controversial subject as stem cell research on the table, it was only minutes until I was embroiled in a polite, but heated exchange.

The kerchief slap came when one woman proudly proclaimed that if she could donate her eggs to create embryos to produce stem cells and a cure for anyone she knew—she would do it. Her boyfriend responded to the apparent generosity of her offer with a nod of approval and a hearty "Amen, sister."

I hesitated to respond, knowing the depths into which such conversations often descend, but nonetheless posited that human life is on a continuum from conception. I explained that from the moment of conception, every human life is genetically human, genetically and sexually distinct, a complete (albeit immature) life form that is able to direct its own growth and development. These characteristics distinguish human life and the embryo from any other clump of cells or tissue produced in or by the body.

I further explained that conception is the only non-arbitrary point at which we can choose to protect human life. Beyond conception, there is no set of human characteristics that even "reasonable" people will agree qualify human life for protection. In other words, there is no logical argument to be made after conception to protect human life at one point that cannot be countered by some other point further along in development.

For example, some argue protection should begin when the heart begins beating at four weeks or when brain waves can be detected at six. Others argue that protection should begin when the face becomes distinguishable at eight weeks or when the child can sense pain at four months. Some think it is the point of viability at 24 weeks—when the child can live independently outside the womb. But that is an ever-moving target, due to advances in technology.

Some people even find it acceptable to take a child's life moments before it is born. And under New Jersey law, it is permissible to kill a child that is created for therapeutic cloning purposes even *after* that child is born. Some renowned academics even suggest that parents should have a few months after the child is born to legally terminate his or her life—kind of like a 90-day money-back guarantee on products not meeting with your satisfaction or approval.

While the dinner guests agreed out loud that the law in New Jersey was ridiculous, they could not see that their position was as arbitrary as the one held by the New Jersey legislators. Nor could they see that their very position opened the door for abortion on demand, the killing of children created through cloning, and even other such common practices as physician-assisted suicide and euthanasia.

Proof of my argument can be easily seen in the Netherlands, where doctors have recently received government-approved guidelines for killing newborn babies—a practice rooted in government-approved euthanasia that started more than 20 years ago.[75]

My opponent's response was to scrape the tip of his knife into a pad of butter, hold it across the table in my direction, and state: "This is not human life."

Never mind the fact that an embryo at three weeks is just about the same size as the butter on his knife and has started to develop recognizable body parts. I realize there is just no getting through to some people.

As an interesting aside: His daughter, who looked to be about 15 or so, became enthralled with my argument and was quite bold in taking the position opposite her dad—a trend among generation Xers that present pro-lifers would be wise to nurture.

To their credit, the whole family attended my presentation the next day. While no obvious conversions took place, they were excited to learn about the alternatives in adult stem cell research. Afterwards, they admitted that it was the more promising and ethical options provided by cord blood and adult stem cell research that made embryonic stem cell research unnecessary and unlikely— another trend that pro-lifers would be wise to nurture.

Denying the basic medical fact that life begins at conception is just another lie used by pro-aborts that has resulted in nothing less than the genocide of an entire generation of children. Did you know that over 3,500 children will die today? Another 3,500 will die tomorrow and the day after that. According to one source, "In the year 2000 alone, "more children died from abortion than Americans died in the Revolutionary War, the Civil War, World Wars I and II the Korean, Vietnam and Gulf Wars combined."[76]

So the answer once again is simple and uncompromising:

L.I.F.E.
Legislate our morality
Identify and deny the lies
Free women from false feminism
End the bloodshed

It is with this simple but effective and instructive acronym that I submit we can win on all three major battlegrounds in the abortion war. Therefore, I charge everyone who recognizes the inherent value of life to take hold of and propagate this message in your own backyard, neighborhood, church, and community. As the saying goes, "It only takes a spark to get a fire going."

Chapter 6

The Duty to Act

N ow what happens if we don't? That is, what will happen if Christians fail to contend for the unborn? Not long ago I participated in a very animated conversation about the role that the Church and church leaders should play in the public square and political arena. The urgency of our discussion became more evident as it coincided with the capitulation of Los Angeles County officials to the American Civil Liberties Union (ACLU) demand that a small cross be removed from the county seal, while the predominant figure, the pagan goddess Pomona, remains.

Generically, our discussion centered on whether church leaders should discuss and advocate action in politics and cultural issues such as prayer in school, pornography, and same-sex marriage.

Immediately, a number of people sounded off with reasons why they should not participate in either. The unifying objection was: "The Church should focus solely on the Gospel message and the saving of lost souls." (And yesss, I attend a Baptist church.)

As I listened to the advocates of this position go on at length, I felt my knuckles tighten around my Bible and whispered to my husband from the side of my mouth, "Say something."

"Before you explode," he replied.

It was too late. I exploded. "The Church and its leaders surely should focus on the Gospel message of Christ—that is the Great Commission, but that is only half the story. The second half is discipleship, which is teaching Christians how to live in a fallen world, and that requires participation in the public square.

"Who can convincingly argue that the state of our nation and its current moral depravity is not intimately linked to the secular mantra that 'Christians should practice their religion in a closet, i.e. STAY OUT of the public square?'

"If church leaders don't provide the rudder *and* the motor on these issues, who will? I mean, we are all so busy running our everyday lives; few have time for plugging into information and action groups outside the Church. We need the Church to help us make the difference we are called to make."

My statement was taken as an affront. One woman responded that her time and sacrifice to the Lord was made in the laundry room, making dinner, and wiping snotty noses. Well, I applaud her. No, really I do. There is *no more valuable place* for women than with their children. Far too many homes have absent parents, and the fallout of a broken home is often devastating. But for this generation to do nothing more than focus on the family means passing a morally bankrupt nation onto our children with clean noses.

Isn't it clear that beyond our duties at home, both the Church and its leaders have a place in the public square? Consider the Scripture in Jude 3-4: "I felt I had to write and urge you to *contend* for the faith that was once for all entrusted to the saints. For certain men whose condemnation was written about long ago have secretly slipped in among you. They are *godless* men, who change the grace of our God into a license for *immorality* and deny Jesus Christ our only Sovereign and Lord" (NIV).

Contend means "to fight, dispute, struggle for and strive." In this context, it means not only for the faith, but against the immorality of godless men. It is here the Church is failing. According to this and other Scripture, we have a duty to fight. Because God made the rules and endowed us with our rights, we are obliged to obey and defend them.

The final response to my argument was that people "appreciate contenders of the 'Christian right,' even if they don't think the Church has a role to play in the public square." To which I would say, "Sure you do." I've worked in ministry for a number of years. Most of those working in ministry are expected to work almost exclusively for Heaven's rewards; never mind about putting food on the table. This is such a sad indictment on the Church that we are not willing to financially support those who daily fight the culture war that is a threat to our very way of life and this nation's founding principles.

That is why the ACLU and other liberal groups frequently go unchallenged by Christians, as in Los Angeles when the ACLU demanded the Cross be removed from the county seal. These secular groups enjoy great support and raise millions of dollars, while Christian groups often struggle to stay afloat and conservative contenders plead for backing.

At the end of the day I don't think church leaders should tell us how to cast our vote, but it is undeniably appropriate to address election issues and platforms as well as any other culturally critical issue impacting our nation. Issues such as presidential elections, Christian symbols, human cloning, abortion, same-sex marriage, pornography, public education, prayer in school, and the Ten Commandments in government buildings are not trivial controversies, but controversies with far-reaching consequences to our way of life.

It is tragic when well-meaning people decide that Christians and their leaders have no role to play in the public square, because when we surrender on issues that are the name, person, and standards of God, we cannot maintain the life and freedoms intended by God in America. Worse, there is a deliberate and methodical movement under way to eradicate the Christian influence and presence from every vestige of life in our nation.

Let me remind us all that the American Revolution, the fight against slavery, crusades to pass child-labor laws, and ban gambling were all led and fought by clergy from the pulpit. Did you know that during the Revolution the black-robed clergy's prominent role in stirring the colonies to fight earned them the name the "Black Regiment" from the British?

That said, I will admit that church leaders today do not have the same freedom of speech from behind the pulpit they once did. Most notably, since Lyndon B. Johnson, faced in 1954 with opposition from non-profit groups, introduced an amendment on the Senate floor to prohibit political activity by tax-exempt organizations, including churches.

The result was that for the first time in American history, political speech from the pulpit was made illegal. Under current federal law, a tax-exempt organization "may not attempt to influence legislation as a substantial part of its activities and it may not participate at all in campaign activity for or against political candidates."[77]

This law has created a "chilling effect" on pulpit-based speakers. Many are intimidated by potential government reprisal, and many do not fully understand the limits of this legislation.

Additionally, most conservatives recognize the widespread distortion of the First Amendment, which has been successfully used as a billy club by liberals to extirpate Christianity from the public square. Witness court rulings removing prayer from schools, the Ten Commandments from government buildings, and Christian symbols from city seals.

The First Amendment reads, in part, "Congress shall make no law respecting an establishment of religion." But prohibiting a government-established church was intended to ensure religious freedom, not eliminate the presence, influence, and voice of the Church from the public square.

The question is: How do we contend for the faith in light of all these restrictions, misinterpretations and influences? Here are my suggestions:

First and foremost, implement the **L.I.F.E.** strategy.

Legislate our morality
Identify and deny the lies
Free women from false feminism
End the bloodshed

Defunding Planned Parenthood is a very good place to start. Find out if your community or state governments help to fund Planned Parenthood and encourage your elected leaders to introduce legislation to prohibit such funding in the future. Also call your elected officials in Washington, D.C., to politely let them know how you feel. Demand better use of your tax dollars and encourage them to sponsor legislation that would remove all government funding from "healthcare" providers that perform abortions.

Second, stay current on the issues. Sign up for *Center Alerts* published by the Center for Reclaiming America for Christ.[78] These alerts are full of important news updates on cultural issues, essential contact information and easy action items for every concerned American.

Third, boldly take responsibility for educating your children about the dangers and consequences of sex outside of marriage. This is a serious matter that extends far beyond the issue of abortion.

Fourth, inform your local school board about the perverse sexual instruction that Planned Parenthood has thrust on other children throughout the nation. Get involved in the fight and their education.

Fifth, and last, consider the following list of action options offered by one mother of four. If you are truly strapped for time—begin the fight in a small manner.

1. All mothers and fathers have the ability to fight with their pocketbooks.

2. If something offends you, SPEAK UP! I took my two youngest to see the *Cat in the Hat* and walked out in 20 minutes, due to the vulgarity and sexual innuendo. I

politely shared my objection with the management and my money was refunded.

3. Compensate for the attack on the public display of Christian symbols by prominently displaying them on your own property. Put a nativity scene in your yard. Buy a Christian flag and fly it on your house. Say grace publicly.

In essence, re-Christianize the atmosphere! None of these suggestions will take away from your family. To the contrary, by getting involved we can secure for them what every parent, every generation hopes to give their children—a better life, with the same liberties and freedoms we enjoyed.

At the beginning of this book I told the tragic story of Christin Gilbert and her baby, who both suffered and died at the hand of an abortionist. What set the story apart from the millions of children and hundreds of women whose lives are ended through abortion is that Christin had Down syndrome. This obviously raises questions about the moral compass of our nation, as well as questions of competence and consent in the decision to abort her child.

Yet what made Christin and her baby special is not the disability. What made Christin and her baby special is what makes us all special—that is the inherent value that comes from being made by God in His image.

The inherent value recognized in a one hundred dollar bill does not change, whether it is crisp and new or crumpled, torn, worn, and old. So it is for every life, regardless of its age and condition. In sharing all this, my personal hope and the hope at the Center for Reclaiming America for Christ is to affirm this simple but powerful truth.

With bold parenting, strong Christian leadership, and support for groups standing on the frontlines, we can win the cultural war. Outside the home the battle to instruct, educate, and contend for the faith belongs to the Church (that would be you and me) and its leaders—both cultural and pastoral. Leaving the battle to the proverbial "others" to fight, with nothing but criticism from the complacent, means we lose on every battlefront and subsequently the broader war on life itself. And lest we forget, the casualties only begin with the 3,500 children aborted each day.

NOTES

1 George Neumay, "The Abortion Debate That Wasn't Under the Radar," American Association of People with Disabilities, July 17, 2005. Available at: http://www.aapd-dc.org/News/disability/abortdebate.html.

2 "Transcript: Day Three of the Roberts Confirmation Hearings," *The Washington Post* (September 14, 2005). Available at: http://www.washingtonpost.com/wp-dyn/content/article/2005/09/14/AR2005091401445.html.

3 "Cause of Death in Texas Teen: 'Complications of Therapeutic Abortion,'" Operation Rescue West, September 14, 2005. Available at: http://www.operationrescue.org/?p=264.

4 Patricia E. Bauer, "The Abortion Debate No One Wants to Have: Prenatal testing is making your right to abort a disabled child more like 'your duty' to abort a disabled child," *The Washington Post* (October 18, 2005), p. A25.

5 "High Amniotic Fluid Levels: Polyhydramnios," American Pregnancy Association, November 2004. Available at: http://www.americanpregnancy.org/labornbirth/highamnioticfluidpolyhydramnios.htm.; Mark H. Beers, M.D. and Robert Berkow, M.D. (eds.), "Congenital anom-

alies: Structural defects present at birth," *The Merck Manual of Diagnosis and Therapy*, Merck Research Laboratories, Whitehouse Station, N.J., 1999. Available at: http://www.merck.com/mrkshared/mmanual/section19/chapter261/261a/jsp.

6 "Man Says He Sold UCLA Body Parts," *CBS News* (March 8, 2004). Available at: http://cbsnews.cbs.com/stories/2004/03/09/national/main604809.shtml; "UCLA apologizes for apparent sale of body parts," CNN (March 8, 2004). Available at: http://www.cnn.com/2004/US/West/03/08/ucla.cadavers/.

7 Woo Suk Hwang et al., "Evidence of a Pluripotent Human Embryonic Stem Cell Line Derived from a Cloned Blastocyst," *Science Express* (February 12, 2004), pp. 1669-74.; Gretchen Vogel, "HUMAN CLONING: Scientists Take Step Toward Therapeutic Cloning," *Science* (February 13, 2004), pp. 937-9.

8 Robert B. Bluey, "New Jersey Governor Under Fire for 'Cloning' Bill," *CNSNews.com* (December 31, 2003). Available at: http://www.cnsnews.com/ViewCulture.asp?Page=%5CCulture%5Carchive%5C200312%5CCUL20031231b.html.; "McGreevey Signs Landmark Stem Cell Research Act," Office of the Governor, January 4, 2004. Available at: http://www.state.nj.us/cgibin/governor/njnewsline/view_article_archives.pl?id=1668.

9 Jim Sedlak, "Planned Parenthood cuts sweetheart deal with producer of 'emergency contraceptive' Plan B," *LifeSiteNews.com* (August 25, 2005). Available at: http://www.lifesite.net/ldn/2005/aug/050825a.html.

10 *Annual Report 2003-2004*, Planned Parenthood Federation of America, Inc., 2004.

11 National Center for Injury Prevention and Control, *Injury Fact Book 2001-2002* (Atlanta, Ga.: Centers for Disease Control and Prevention, 2001), 6. Available at: http://www.cdc.gov/ncipc/fact_book/04_Introduction.htm; National Center for Health Statistics, *Health, United States, 2004 with Chartbook on Trends in the Health of Americans* (Hyattsville, Md.: U.S. Department for Health and Human Services, 2004), 154. Available at: http://www.cdc.gov/nchs/products/pubs/pubd/hus/ 2010/2010.htm#hus02.

12 *Cancer Facts & Figures 2003*, (Atlanta, Ga.: American Cancer Society, Inc., 2003). Available at: http://www.cancer.org/downloads/ STT/CAFF2003PWSecured.pdf.

13 Centers for Disease Control and Prevention, *National diabetes fact sheet: general information and national estimates on diabetes in the United States,* 2003, (Atlanta, Ga.: U.S. Department of Health and Human Services, Centers for Disease Control and Prevention, 2004). Available at: http://www.cdc.gov/diabetes/pubs/estimates.htm.

14 "Auto deaths decline," *CNN Money* (August 1, 2005). Available at: http://money.cnn.com/2005/08/01/Autos/nhtsa_death_stats/.

15 "Mortality Declines for Several Leading Causes of Death in 1999," Centers for Disease Control and Prevention, June 26, 2001. Available at: http://www.cdc.gov/od/oc/media/pressrel/r010626.htm.

16 Centers for Disease Control and Prevention, *HIV/AIDS Surveillance Report: HIV Infection and AIDS in the United States, 2003,* Vol. 15, (Atlanta, Ga.: U.S. Department of Health and Human Services, Centers for Disease Control and Prevention, 2004). Available at: http://www.cdc.gov/hiv/stats/2003SurveillanceReport.htm.

17 *Annual Report 2003-2004*, Planned Parenthood Federation of America, Inc., 2004.

18 Ibid.; *Annual Report 2002-2003*, Planned Parenthood Federation of America, Inc., 2003.; Original sources for cited material available from "Detailed financial data for Planned Parenthood's last five years," STOPP International. Available at: http://www.all.org/stopp/fdlast5y/htm.

19 Ibid.; Ibid., Planned Parenthood Federation of America, Inc., 2003.; Original sources for cited material available from "Detailed service data for Planned Parenthood's last five years," STOPP International. Available at: http://www.all.org/stopp/sdlast5y/htm.

20 Original sources for cited material available from the Center for Reclaiming America for Christ website: http://www.reclaimamerica.org/pages/campaigns/PPH/PPHFinancial Overview.pdf.

21 Ibid.

22 "Fact Sheet: Department of Homeland Security Appropriations Act of 2005," The Department of Homeland Security, October 18, 2004. Available at: http://www.dhs.gov/dhspublic/interapp/press_release/press_release_0541.xml.

23 Ibid.

24 "2004 Presidential Election," Center for Responsive Politics. Available at: http://www.opensecrets.org/presidential/index.asp.

25 Cited by Wanda Franz, "Rankings and Reality," *National Right to Life News* (December 1999). Available at:http://www.nrlc.org/news/1999/NRL1299/pres.html.

26 Tom Strode, "Judge strikes down partial-birth abortion ban, says law places 'undue burden' on women," *Baptist Press News* (June 1, 2004). Available at: http://www.bpnews.net/bpnews.asp?ID=18379.

27 Charles Lane, "Justices to Hear N.H. Abortion Notification Challenge," *The Washington Post* (May 24, 2005), p. A6. Available at: http://www.washingtonpost.com/wp-dyn/content/article/2005/05/23/AR2005052300599.html.

28 Original sources for the cited information available from the Center for Reclaiming America for Christ website: http://www.reclaimamerica.org/pages/campaigns/PPH/PPHFinancial Overview.pdf.

29 Maria Gallagher, "South Dakota State Library Removes Web Site Link to Planned Parenthood," *LifeNews.com* (July 13, 2004). Available at: http://www.lifenews.com/state641.html.

30 "Ask the Experts," Planned Parenthood Federation of America, October 9, 2003. Available at: http://www.teenwire.com/ask/2003/as_20031009p660_semen.asp.

31 "Ask the Experts," Planned Parenthood Federation of America, July 10, 2001. Available at: http://www.teenwire.com/ask/2001/as-20010710p244.php.; "Ask the Experts," Planned Parenthood Federation of America, April 25, 2003. Available at: http://www.teenwire.com/ask/2003/as-20030425p552-anal.php.

32 "Ask the Experts," Planned Parenthood Federation of America, October 6, 2005. Available at: http://www.teenwire.com/ask/2005/as-20051006p1129-anus.php.

33 Elisa Klein, "Losing It: All About Virginity," *In Focus*, Planned

Parenthood Federation of America, April 13, 2004. Available at: http://www.teenwire.com/infocus/2004/if-20040413p282-virginity.php.

34 Minna Dubin, "Are You Experienced?" *In Focus*, Planned Parenthood Federation of America, June 8, 2004. Available at: http://www.teenwire.com/infocus/2004/if-20040608p296-experience.php.

35 Cited in "What Planned Parenthood Leaders Say," Life Decisions International. Available at: http://www.fightpp.org/show.cfm?page=leaders.

36 *Groovy New Feelings*, Canadian Federation for Sexual Health, December 6, 2004. Available at: http://www.ppfc.ca/ppfc/content.asp?articleid=351.

37 "Planned Parenthood gives kids 'porn' book," *World Net Daily* (July 17, 2004). Available at: http://www.wnd.com/news/article.asp?ARTICLE_ID=39498.

38 "Condom Necklace Sparks Outrage at Fair," *Associated Press* (July 24, 2004). Available at: http://www.phillyburbs.com/pb-dyn/articlePrint.cfm?id=336346.

39 "Ratings: Condoms," *Consumer Reports* (February 2005). Available at: http://www.consumerreports.org/cro/health-fitness/health-care/condoms-and-contraception-205/ratings.htm.

40 "Facts in Brief: Induced Abortion in the United States," Guttmacher Institute, May 18, 2005. Available at: http://www.agi-usa.org/pubs/fb_induced_abortion.html.

41 Susan Jones, "'Does Size Matter,' Asks Ruler Sold by Abortion

Provider, *CNS News* (August 6, 2004). Available at:
http://www.cnsnews.com/ViewCulture.asp?Page=%5CCulture
%5Carchive%5C200408%5CCUL20040806b.html.

42 "'I had an Abortion' – Pride T-shirts available from Planned
Parenthood," *LifeSiteNews.com* (July 23, 2004). Available at:
http://www.lifesite.net/ldn/2004/jul/04072304.html.

43 Original sources for cited material available from the Center for
Reclaiming America for Christ website:
http://www.reclaimamerica.org/pages/campaigns/PPH/
PPHFinancialOverview.pdf.

44 Dr. Jill Ker Conway, "Studying Women's Lives," *Harvard
University Extension School Alumni Bulletin* (Fall 1999). Available at:
http://drclas.fas.harvard.edu/index.pl/programs/art_forum/bermudez?
proxiedUrl=http%3A%2F%2Fwww.dce.harvard.edu%2Fpubs%2Falu
m%2F1999%2F02.html&wid=257&func=view.; Margaret Sanger,
Margaret Sanger, An Autobiography (New York: W. W. Norton,
1938), 86-7.

45 Original source for cited information available at http://
blackgenocide.org/sanger.html.

46 "The Truth About Margaret Sanger," Planned Parenthood
Federation of America, Inc. Available at: http://www.plannedparent-
hood.org/pp2/portal/files/portal/medicalinfo/birthcontrol/bio-
margaret-sanger.xml.

47 Laurie D. Elam-Evans, Ph.D. et al., *Abortion Surveillance—
United States, 2000*, Centers for Disease Control and Prevention
(November 28, 2003). Available at: http://www.cdc.gov/mmwr/
preview/mmwrhtml/ss5212a1.htm.

48 *Dred Scott v. Sanford,* 60 U.S. 393, 407 (1857).

49 Tanya L. Green, "The Negro Project: Margaret Sanger's Eugenic Plan for Black Americans," Life Education and Resource Network Northeast Chapter, BLACKGENOCIDE.ORG. Available at http://blackgenocide.org/negro06.html.

50 B.V. Stadel et al., "Oral contraceptives and breast cancer in young women," *The Lancet* (February 22, 1986), p. 436.

51 H.L. Howe et al., "Annual report to the nation on the status of cancer, 1973 through 1998, featuring cancers with recent increasing trends," *Journal of the National Cancer Institute* (2001), pp. 824-42.; Karen Malec, "The Abortion-Breast Cancer Link: How Politics Trumped Science and Informed Consent," *Journal of American Physicians and Surgeons* (Summer 2003), p. 41. Available at: http://www.jpands.org/vol8no2/malec.pdf

52 Vanessa Cullins, "Ask Dr. Cullins: Does having an abortion really lead to breast cancer?" *choice! Magazine,* Planned Parenthood Federation of America. Available at: http://www.plannedparenthood.org/pp2/portal/files/portal/webzine/askdrcullins/adc-030425-abortion.xml.

53 "About Komen." Accessed at http://www.komen.org/intradoc-cgi/idc_cgi_isapi.dll?IdcService=SS_GET_PAGE&nodeId=299.

54 "Appeals Court Lifts Injunction Preventing Texas From Withholding Federal Funds From Groups That Provide Abortions," *Medical News Today* (March 20, 2005). Available at: http://www.medicalnewstoday.com/medicalnews.php?newsid=21545.

55 Greg Cunningham, "Some Area Health Services Cut," *Amarillo*

Globe-News (November 9, 2003). Available at: http://www.amarillo.com/stories/110903/new_healthcut.shtml.

56 Anna Lindsay, "Parents' joy as Charlotte goes home," BBC News, Portsmouth, UK, December 7, 2005: http://news.bbc.co.uk/2/hi/uk_news/england/hampshire/4502658.stm#

57 *Medical Decisions About the End of Life, I. Report of the Committee to Study the Medical Practice Concerning Euthanasia. II. The Study for the Committee on Medical Practice Concerning Euthanasia* (2 vols.), The Hague, September 19, 1991. Report I, p. 15. Cited in "Euthanasia in the Netherlands," International Task Force on Euthanasia and Assisted Suicide. Accessed at http://www.internationaltaskforce.org/fctholl.htm.

58 "Medical end-of-life decisions made for neonates and infants in the Netherlands," van der Heide A, et.al., *The Lancet,* Vol. 350, Issue 9073, 26 July 1997, Pages 251-255; "End-of-life decisions in Dutch paediatric practice," van der Heide A, et al. *Lancet* - Vol. 350, Issue 9092, 6 December 1997, Page 1711; Wesley J. Smith, "Now They Want to Euthanize Children," *The Weekly Standard* (September 13, 2004) http://www.weeklystandard.com/Content/Public/Articles/000/000/004/616jszlg.asp

59 "From euthanasia to infanticide: The Dutch approach to severely sick newborns," *National Catholic Register* (March 28 – April 3, 2005). Accessed at http://www.citizenimpact.ca/issues/euthanasia_prevention/euthanasia_infanticide.html

60 Furrow, BA et al., *Bioethics; Health Care Law and Ethics,* fifth edition. (West Publishing Co. 2004) p.222-226.

61 Misdiagnosis of Terri Schiavo exposed on *Hannity & Colmes:*

Michael Schiavo's abusive behavior also revealed, transcript from *Hannity & Colmes*, Fox News Channel, March 22, 2005, and RenewAmerica staff, March 23, 2005. http://www.renewamerica.us/news/050323hannity.htm; *Robert and Mary Schindler v Michael Schiavo*, guardian of the person of Theresa Marie Schindler Schiavo petition to the Florida Supreme Court to reverse Judge Greer's refusal to reinsert the PEG tube. http://www.miami.edu/ethics2/schiavo/timeline.htm March 26, 2005; Florida S.Ct. Order refusal to reinsert feeding tube due to lack of jurisdiction, March 26, 2005, Case no: SC05-497. http://www.miami.edu/ethics2/schiavo/032605%20Fla%20S%20Ct%20Order.pdf

62 Do No Harm Fact Sheet: "Benefits of Stem Cells to Human Patients - Adult Stem Cells vs. Embryonic Stem Cells." Updated July 19, 2005 http://www.stemcellresearch.org/facts/treatments.htm

63 K-S Kang et al., "A 37-year-old spinal cord-injured female patient, transplanted of multipotent stem cells from human UC blood, with improved sensory perception and mobility, both functionally and morphologically: a case study" *Cytotherapy*, Volume 7, Number 4, September 2005, pp. 368-373.

64 Kodama S, Kühtreiber W, Fujimura S, Dale EA, Faustman DL. "Islet regeneration during the reversal of autoimmune diabetes in NOD mice." *Science.* 2003; 302 (5648):1223-7; Ryu S, Kodama S, Ryu K, Schoenfeld DA, Faustman DL. "Reversal of established autoimmune diabetes by restoration of endogenous beta cell function." *Journal of Clinical Investigation.* 2001 Jul;108(1):63-72; "Updates from Dr. Faustman's Laboratory at Massachusetts General Hospital"; Issue Fall 2005 http://www.joinleenow.org/downloads/FaustmanUpdate_Fall05.pdf

65 A study showed that embryonic stem cells produced insulin-producing cells, again not beta cells, and they did not cure the mice but formed tumors. Sipione S., et al., "Insulin expressing cells from differentiated embryonic stem cells are not beta cells," *Diabetologia* 47, 499-508, 2004 (published online February 14, 2004).

66 Phone conversation on December 9, 2005, with Lee Allen, Director of Communications at the National Council for Adoption.

67 Mark Crutcher, *On Message: Understanding and Communicating the Pro-life Position* (Life Dynamics Inc., 2005), pp 88-90.

68 "Recidivism of Sex Offenders," Center for Sex Offender Management. A project of the Office of Justice Programs, U.S. Department of Justice May 2001. Accesssed at http://www.csom.org/pubs/recidsexof.html

69 *The Worst Experiences Create Some of the Best People* — Oprah Winfrey's Story, THRIVEnet Story of the Month-April, 1997: http://www.thrivenet.com/stories/stories97/stry9704.html

70 "Abortion-List Grab Battle Heats Up WASHINGTON," March 23, 2005 CBS NEWS Healthwatch http://www.cbsnews.com/stories/2005/03/23/health/main682683.shtml

71 "Study: Movies with explicit sex don't sell: 63% of top films in past 3 years had moral or Christian worldview," WorldNetDaily.com. Posted: March 26, Accessed at 2004http://worldnetdaily.com/news/article.asp?ARTICLE_ID=37746

72 "Internet Pornography Statistics," Jerry Ropelato, *Internet Filter Review,* 2005 TopTenREVIEWS, Inc. http://internet-filter-review.toptenreviews.com/internet-pornography-statistics.html

73 Testimony for U.S. Senate Committee on Commerce, Science and Transportation, March 4, 1999, Mary Anne Layden, Ph.D., Director of Education, Center for Cognitive Therapy, University of Pennsylvania. http://commerce.senate.gov/hearings/0304lay.pdf)

74 Gissler M, Kauppila R, Merlainen J, Toukomaa H, Hemminki E, Pregnancy-associated deaths in Finland 1987-1994: register linkage study, *British Medical Journal,* 1996 December 7; 313(7070):1431-4. Statistics and citations taken from a compilation of studies in: *Women's Health after Abortion: the Medical and Psychological Evidence* by Elizabeth Ring-Cassidy and Ian Gentles. Published by the Toronto based de Veber Institute for Bioethics and Social Research 2002. Page 52 makes a very important note on this highly politicized issue: "There is a marked tendency in the North-American literature on abortion for researchers to minimize their own findings. Those interested in the subject are well advised to read the numerical data and compare them carefully with the abstract or conclusions, rather than relying on either the abstract or conclusions alone. Comparisons are also recommended with literature from European countries, particularly Great Britain and the Scandinavian countries, where population size and sophisticated medical linkage data bases make data collection more accurate and comprehensive."; Medical and Psychological Talking Points "Why Women Deserve Better than Abortion," *Feminists For Life* 2004. http://www.feministsforlife.org/WDB/talkingpoints.htm

75 "Dutch to set guidelines for euthanasia of babies," Associated Press (September 29, 2005). Accessed http://www.msnbc.msn.com/id/9532252/; Emma Thomasson, "Dutch commission to set rules on baby euthanasia," Reuters (November 29, 2005). Accessed at

http://www.msnbc.msn.com/id/10249698/from/RL.1/

76 National Right to Life Issue Information, "Abortion in the United States: Statistics and Trends." Estimate of 1,312,990 U.S. abortions for 2000. Accessed at

http://www.nrlc.org/abortion/facts/abortionstats.html

77 Internal Revenue Service, United States Department of the Treasury, "Charitable Organizations Exemption Requirements," Accessed at

http://www.irs.gov/charities/charitable/article/0,,id=96099,00.html.

78 To sign up for *Center Alerts* from the Center for Reclaiming America for Christ, go to http://www.cfra.info/153/petition.asp.